A RotoVision Book in Collaboration with
GREY PRESS, Berlin

Published and distributed by RotoVision SA
7 Rue du Bugnon
1299 Crans
Switzerland

RotoVision SA Sales Office
Sheridan House
112/116 A Western Road
Hove, East Sussex
BN3 1DD, England
Tel +44 (0)1273 72 72 68
Fax +44 (0)1273 72 72 69
E.Mail sales@rotovision.com

Distributed to the trade in the United States by
Watson-Guptill Publications
1515 Broadway
New York, NY 10036

ISBN 2-88046-329-7

Text
Veruschka Götz

Design
Ben Erben, London
Veruschka Götz, Berlin

English translation
Victor Dewsbery, Berlin

Thanks to
Tobias Hellmann, David Krebs,
Anja Nolle & Sandra Nodes,
Markus Beauchamp

Production and separations in Singapore by
ProVision Pte Ltd.
Tel +65 334 77 20
Fax +65 334 77 21

color & type
for the screen

List of Contents

INTRODUCTION

digital stuttering

At the beginning of the 20th century, the horse-drawn carriage gave way to the automobile. Despite the obvious differences between the two forms of transport, there remained for a long time a marked similarity between the first automobiles and their horse-drawn predecessors. It was only after a slow and gradual process that automobile design shook off the legacy of the past and began fully to reflect the potential and requirements of the new technology.

For example, with the greater speed of the new vehicles, it was no longer possible to travel over cobbled roads on wooden wheels. The answer, of course, was pneumatic tyres which are still used today, having themselves been constantly adapted to keep pace with the progress of technology. When, as sometimes happens, a the computer monitor is a completely different medium from paper.

Whereas text printed on paper is a solid object, text on the computer screen is based on light waves. These create the white background and the black text results from an absence of light.

Thus, most of the screen desktop consists of light rays which after a time will become irritating to the eye as well as completely exhausting. This has consequences for the use of typography on the screen.

Even newsprint offers a better resolution than text presented on the screen. What works on paper cannot be simply transferred to the computer monitor.

So there is no point in trying to impose on the computer the

color & type

color

process of gradual improvement suddenly results in a completely new invention, it may not be possible for the new product to obey the old laws. So, in using color and type on the computer screen, the old rules governing printing on paper no longer apply. In everyday use, the general rule is to use black print on plain white paper, for example in business correspondence, books and newsletters. With the computer screen too, it is common to have a white background with black text.

Yet this fails to take into account that techniques of the old printing technology; the result will be an inappropriate design that will make the viewer "stutter" as he or she reads. This book aims to help improve design for the computer screen in order to produce text that is attractive and easy to read.

Color & Type for the Screen does not set up inflexible rules for the use of colour and typography on the computer. Its intention is simply to make some suggestions and help the reader to develop an awareness of some of the issues.

Hopefully, one day technology will advance to the point where it will no longer be necessary to settle for some of the compromise solutions suggested below.

Rules relating to typography and color on paper do not necessarily apply on the computer screen, but they do represent a frame of reference, and they provide a vocabulary and a starting point.

The issue of legibility highlights the difference between design in print and on the computer screen, in particular in relation to the selection of typography and to type sizes, tracking, and the use of line lengths and line spaces. Typefaces which were generally designed for print media pose problems when used on modern 72 dpi monitors. The type has to also be above a certain point size, and a wider tracking value than in print media must be used to make the text easy to read.

So while screen design can, of course, be regarded as a matter of taste, there are limits to what is possible, and

anything goes?

In theory everything is possible. Texts are of course written to be read, and use language as a form of communication, but to the creative designer type is just a visual element and typography an art form. So the designer must decide whether he or she wants to make the text legible, and thus comprehensible, or whether his or her priority is the abstract attractiveness of the design. And, while experiments are important in order to extend and improve the existing rules, it is important to know the existing rules in order to lay them aside and judge what is new.

It is a matter of choice whether the content of the text is the main priority.

some solutions work better than others. Above all, it is vital to recognise that the computer is a separate medium in its own right. It should be treated accordingly – taking its weaknesses into account, using its strengths, and rethinking our approach to visual perception. Above all, design for the screen should not simply be based on what works with design on paper.

& type   color & type

2

COLORS

colors

Two of the major systems in color theory are the additive and subtractive systems.

The additive color system uses combinations of red, green, and blue to make up the colors of the spectrum. A mixture of different colors, will be interpreted by the brain as a single color. The same applies when different color dots are so close together that the eye is unable to see them as separate.

When the three primary colors of red, green, and blue are of equal intensity, they mix to make up a pure white. When two primary colors overlap, a third color is produced, a so-called secondary color.

When red and green are mixed, they produce yellow.

When red and blue are mixed, the result is purple (magenta).

Blue and green make up cyan blue (cyan).

This additive color system is used, for example, in the reproduction of colors on the computer screen. It is referred to as the RGB model, from the initial letters of the three primary colors.

The subtractive color system consists of the primary colors of cyan, magenta, and yellow. When these colors are mixed in equal intensity, they produce black.

But mixing the three primary colors of cyan, magenta, and yellow does not produce a really deep black – it is more like a dark brown – so extra black is added. This system is known by the abbreviation CMYK (cyan, magenta, yellow, key color) and it forms the basis of the printing process.

Red, green, and blue are the primary colors in the additive color system. Cyan, magenta, and yellow are the secondary colors. Red, green, and blue together make up white.

Cyan, magenta, and yellow are the primary colors in the subtractive color system. Red, green, and blue are the secondary colors. Cyan, magenta, and yellow together make up black.

Magenta

Cyan

Black

Yellow

Red
R=100%
G=0%
B=0%

White

Blue
R=0%
G=0%
B=100%

Green
R=0%
G=100%
B=0%

The same color, when displayed on two different computer screens, may in fact look different – depending on the standards used for the primary colors.

Color and Type

Color and Type

Color and Type

Color and Type

Color and Type

Color and Type

Color mixtures

Blue and green = cyan
Red and blue = magenta
Red and green = yellow

Yellow and cyan = green
Magenta and cyan = blue
Yellow and magenta = red

colors as a screen background

Red

active	aggressive
invigorating	
exciting	
powerful	
strong	
energetic	
attractive	
dominating	

Pink

caring
sweet
tender

Violet

masculine	inhibiting
exciting (red)	gloomy (blue)
mystical	lonely
sensual	murky
enchanting	agitated
delicate	

Blue

controlled	
abstinent	
mysterious	
intellectual	
harmonious	aggressive
introverted	
cold	
melancholy	
deep	
dreamy	
faithful	
rational	
sensible	

Blue-green / turquoise

	aloof
	self-willed
refreshing	unemotional
	cold
	sterile

Light green

stimulating	hectic
	poisonous
	compulsive

Green

refreshing
harmonious
optimistic
close to nature
calm
gentle
conciliatory
strong-willed

Lemon yellow

	dangerous
	poisonous
refreshing	sickly
	artificial
	nervous
	annoyed

It is important to choose the screen background color very carefully, since it is generally the largest single area of color. Such criteria as color character, color brightness, and the colors of the other elements, all need to be taken into consideration.

It is important to be clear in advance what effect is being sought.

The screen background color is seldom the only color on the screen.

It is usually combined with type, symbols, pictures, or logos.

These different elements interact and provide each other with quantity and quality contrast. (Quantity contrast refers to the size of the areas covered by the colors; quality contrast describes the color contrast itself.)

For example, red appears far more intense when placed alongside black than it does when combined with violet.

Colors are neither good nor bad in themselves, but they do have a positive or negative, conscious or unconscious psychological effect on the viewer, depending on his or her subjective experience and moods. Yellow, for example, is usually rejected by people who are ill. In fact, though yellow can prompt a variety of responses, depending on the shade. A greenish yellow can suggest envy and deceitfulness.

A reddish yellow may be thought of as cheerful, colorful, and lively. But a vivid yellow is sometimes regarded as provocative and self-assertive.
The only constant seems to be the color's stimulating effect.
Likewise rich middle red, which is another very stimulating color, can stand for love and vitality, or equally well for aggression, terror, or revolution. A more yellowish red will seem cheerful and powerful, but with shades of pink it will appear sweet and more recessive.

When choosing an area of color for the screen, the intrinsic brightness of the individual color is another vital factor, and a decision must also be made as to how much light the eyes can stand.

The atmospheric mood that is produced by a color is a vitally important aspect to consider. The color circle propounded by the German writer Johann Wolfgang von Goethe divides colors into a "plus and minus side".
This refers to a distinction between colors which stimulate actively and those which are perceived passively. Red, yellow, and orange, which Goethe described as lively and aspiring, are considered active, while shades of blue and violet are usually thought passive. The choice between stimulating and relaxing colors is just one of an infinite number of options facing the designer. Another is the degree of warmth. The graduations from yellow to red, for example represent a gradual increase in warmth.
Warm colors as a screen background are likely to stimulate and excite the viewer.
An intense red increases the pulse and heart rate, for example whereas blue has the opposite effect. Studies have even shown that time seems to pass more slowly under intense blue radiation. White light, on the other hand, increases alertness but uses up energy more quickly, so that the viewer quickly becomes tired. It is essential therefore to ask what mood should the design of a screen background is intended to create.

Yellow

colorful	superficial
extrovert	exaggerated
cheerful	vain
youthful	
lively	
full of fun	
light	

Orange

exciting	intimate
direct	vigorous
joyful	possessive
alive	
communicative	
warm	

Dark red

graceful
serious
dignified

17

colors as a screen background

Any judgement of colors is bound to be relative, because the environment of a color affects the way it is perceived. The same color can have totally different effects in different environments.

Color and Type
Color and Type

Color and Type
Color and Type

Black

elegant
firm

aloof
inflexible
sad
negative
reserved

Color and Type
Color and Type

White

affirmative
open
pure
uninhibited

Color and Type
Color and Type

Gray

neutral

unemotional
joyless
empty

Color and Type
Color and Type

Color and Type
Color and Type

Red, for example, can appear bright,
when in combination with black,
but can seem completely dull when it
is combined with orange.

Colors interact with each other. Yellow
changes its mood, and to some extent
its actual hue, depending on the color
combination.

Yellow and black in combination form
the greatest contrast between
chromatic and achromatic. The mood
is one of alarm and danger.

The same yellow in combination with
green has a completely different
feeling: close to nature and relaxed
because the colors are close together
in the color circle.

Yellow and blue, which are opposite
each other in the color circle, form an
exciting contrast.
The result is balanced comprehensive
and complementary (like day and night).

light waves

Human color vision, i.e. the ability to distinguish colors irrespective of their brightness, is controlled by rods in the eye.

The human eye has three types of rods, each of which reacts most strongly to one of the three primary colors in the additive color system: red, blue (blue-violet), and green.

In the spectrum of light, only light with a wavelength between 380nm and 780nm (1nm = 1 billionth of a metre) appears as a color to the human eye. Within this range, the human being can perceive up to 7 million color valences.

The range of color sensations all result from a mixture of the three primary colors. The sensitivity of the three different types of rods overlaps, so that for a range of about 500 mm the green-sensitive rod reacts most strongly, but the red-sensitive and blue-sensitive rods also react to a lesser extent. The actual visual impression in the brain is made up of a combination of the stimuli from all three types of rods. This is why human beings can see more colors than the continuous spectrum shows.

For example, there is no uniform frequency for the colors of brown or gray. They are "artificial" products of the brain which result from the stimuli of the different rods. If all three types of rod are stimulated to an equal extent, the result is a sensation of white. If the green-sensitive rods and the red-sensitive rods are excited in a certain ratio, the result is a sensation of yellow.

Blue-violet corresponds to a wavelength of 380nm, red corresponds to a wavelength of 780nm. Ultra-violet, which has a wavelength that is smaller than 380nm, is outside the range of human vision.

The light rays which have the greatest effect on the eye, and thus those which seem the most intense, are those with a wavelength of about 555nm, which corresponds to a yellow-green. The red-sensitive and green-sensitive rods are most sensitive at this wavelength. A further factor is that the red-sensitive and green-sensitive rods react more sensitively than the blue-sensitive rods.

When blue is compared with other colors which are of the same brightness but more in the range of the red-sensitive or green-sensitive rods, it will appear less intense.

**Relative
Sensitivity**

- ■ Blue-sensitive cone
- ■ Green-sensitive cone
- ■ Red-sensitive cone

380 450 500 555 600 660 780 nm

**Relative
Sensitivity**

Range / Field no
longer visible to
the human eye

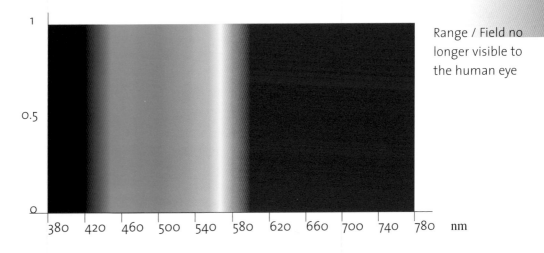

Range / Field no
longer visible to
the human eye

380 420 460 500 540 580 620 660 700 740 780 nm

brightness of colors

Colors on the screen always appear slightly artificial. This is because colors on screen are made up of light rather than color pigments, as they are when printed on paper. Our natural color perception habits are adapted to richly - saturated colors, and the computer screen is unable to present these with the same intensity. If we compare a color from a printed color scale with the same color on the screen, the screen version always appears paler and more unreal.

Each color has an intrinsic brightness. This intrinsic brightness in a saturated form, i.e. not lightened with white, makes a color appear striking or restrained.
If the intrinsic brightness of the type is identical to, or only slightly different from, the brightness of the background, it will be hard to read.
It is therefore best to avoid harmonic color combinations with the same brightness. To make texts easier to read, it is possible to use contrasting colors. But these contrasts should be selected to avoid combinations of "pure" colors, or the result will be glaring and over-colorful. The contrasts in the intrinsic brightness should also not be too extreme, because this can easily lead to flickering on the screen, much more easily than would happen with the same color combinations on paper.

Creating a contrast by using a darkened background color combined with light-colored type is one attractive solution. If the background color selected for the screen is too bright, it may "bloom over" a darker type.

Color and Type
Color and Type

This gray and this blue are almost equal in their intrinsic brightness.

Color and Type
Color and Type

The purer a color is, the more sparingly it should be used.

Color and Type
Color and Type

Black and this blue have almost the same intrinsic brightness.

Color and Type
Color and Type

The intrinsic brightness of the green has been reduced.

This table shows a summary of different colors in relation to their intrinsic brightness.
It does not include mixed shades brightened or darkened by adding white, or black or finer shades arising from combinations of colors.

A mixture of green with a large proportion of yellow gives the green a completely different appearance. If a color with a medium intrinsic brightness is mixed with a color with a high intrinsic brightness, it will take on a higher brightness value.

	Achromatic colors	Colors	Intrinsic brightness
100	White		Very high
		Yellow, yellow-green	High
		Orange	High to medium
	Medium gray	Red, green	Medium
		Violet	Medium to low
		Blue	Low
0	Black		None

colors and contrasts

When looking at a computer screen, there sometimes seems to be a continuous flickering. When this happens, it means the contrast between the background and the type needs to be reduced. For example, it is best to avoid strong color contrasts such as the use of contrasting complementary colors, black and white contrasts and strong contrasts, between chromatic and achromatic colors.

The first area to consider is the design of the screen surface. (Here it is advisable to reduce the distance between the viewer and screen.) The first thing to consider is the actual color of the screen itself, rather than any additional working surface created on the screen:

Black

A black screen background is much easier on the eyes and more user-friendly because flickering will be kept to the absolute minimum. But when selecting colors, the screen designer also needs to consider their psychology and many users feel that a black background is extremely sombre, or even depressing.

On black paper, white type appears narrower than the usual "black on white". However, when white type is displayed on a black screen background, the opposite applies.

Color and Type
Color and Type

Background 100% black, type white

Color and Type
Color and Type

Background 10% black, type 100%black

White type on a black screen background also looks bolder than black type on a white screen background, because of the "blooming" effect the white on the screen is not a material substance, as with a sheet of paper, but light. A possible solution is to display the type in 5 – 10 % black, and thus to minimize the blooming.

Color and Type
Color and Type

Background 100% black, type 10% black

At these percentage color values, the viewer still has the impression that he or she is looking at white type. Once the percentage exceeds 15%, the type appears gray. Gray text is clearly legible between 20% and 50% black. Above 60% black, the type is difficult to distinguish from the black background.

Color and Type
Color and Type

Background 100% black, type 30% black

Color and Type
Color and Type

Background 100% black, type 40% black

Color and Type
Color and Type

Background 100% black, type 5% black

Color and Type
Color and Type

Background 100% black, type 50% black

Color and Type
Color and Type

Background 100% black, type 15% black

Color and Type
Color and Type

Background 100% black, type 60% black

Color and Type
Color and Type

Background 100% black, type 20% black

Color and Type
Color and Type

Background 100% black, type 70% black

Color and Type
Color and Type

Background 100% black, type 80% black

colors and contrasts

Color and Type

Geneva, black 30 %, 20 pt

Color and Type
Color and Type
Color and Type
Color and Type
Color and Type
Color and Type

Geneva, black 5 %, 11 pt
Geneva, black 15 %
Geneva, black 30 %
Geneva, black 40 %
Geneva, black 50 %
Geneva, black 60 %

Color and **Type**

Balanced, Geneva, black,
normal 5 %, bold 15 %, 11 pt

Color and Type

Balanced, Geneva, black
normal 5 % , bold 10 %, 20 pt

The percentage values for light-colored type on a black background are meant as a guideline. The smaller the size of the type, the darker the type appears, even with the same percentage values. The same also applies to different fonts of the same typeface. The thinner the font selected, the darker the type appears in comparison with bolder fonts.

When using larger type sizes (20pt and above) higher color percentages will be needed to create the same color impression as was obtained with smaller type. This is important, for example, in adapting headings to match the body type.

To obtain a balanced color impression when using thin, normal and bold fonts in body text of the same size, it may be necessary to change the percentage values for the colors. This must be done individually, depending on the size and font used.

In a comparison on the screen, black type on a white or very light-colored background will look smaller than white type on a black background. This is the exact opposite of the effect on paper.

Color and Type

Geneva, red 30 %, 20 pt

Color and Type
Color and Type
Color and Type
Color and Type
Color and Type
Color and Type

Geneva, black 50 %, 10 pt
Geneva, black 60 %
Geneva, black 70 %
Geneva, black 80 %
Geneva, black 90 %
Geneva, black 100 %

Taking the normal font as standard, it will be necessary to reduce the percentage value of the color for thinner fonts and increase it for bolder fonts. The smaller the size of the type, the more the color value will need to be adjusted. As the example shows, with 11 pt type on a black background, the percentage value of the black for a normal font is 5%, and for a bold font it is 15%.

20 pt type has a black percentage of 5% for the normal font, 10% for the bold font.
In the example of red type on a black background, it is clear again that a smaller type size appears darker than a larger size.
Here, too, the color percentage values in the lower example had to be adapted to obtain the same color impression.

Color and Type

Geneva, red 40 %, 20 pt

Color and Type — Geneva, red 5 %, 11 pt
Color and Type — Geneva, red 15 %
Color and Type — Geneva, red 30 %
Color and Type — **Geneva, red 40 %**
Color and Type — Geneva, red 50 %
Color and Type — Geneva, red 60 %

Color and Type

Balanced, Geneva, red,
normal 60 %, bold 75 %, 11 pt

Color and Type

Balanced, Geneva, red,
normal 60 %, bold 65 %, 20 pt

achromatic contrasts

Here the percentage value for the type remains the same, while the background changes.

Here the percentage values for the type have been adapted so the type appears white, while the background changes.

Color and Type
Color and Type

Background black 100 %,
Geneva black 20 %, 20 pt, 11 pt

Color and Type
Color and Type

Background black 90 %,
Geneva black 15 %, 20 pt, 11 pt

Color and Type
Color and Type

Background black 90 %,
Geneva black 20 %, 20 pt, 11 pt

Color and Type
Color and Type

Background black 80 %,
Geneva black 15 %, 20 pt, 11 pt

Color and Type
Color and Type

Background black 80 %,
Geneva black 20 %, 20 pt, 11 pt

Color and Type
Color and Type

Background black 70 %,
Geneva black 10 %, 20 pt, 11 pt

Color and Type
Color and Type

Background black 70 %,
Geneva black 20 %, 20 pt, 11 pt

Color and Type
Color and Type

Background black 60 %,
Geneva black 10 %, 20 pt, 11 pt

Color and Type
Color and Type

Background black 60 %,
Geneva black 20 %, 20 pt, 11 pt

Color and Type
Color and Type

Background black 50 %,
Geneva black 5 %, 20 pt, 11 pt

Color and Type
Color and Type

Background black 50 %,
Geneva black 20 %, 20 pt, 11 pt

Achromatic contrast offers a simple way of producing easily legible text on the screen with a minimum of strain to the eyes, using black as a basis for both the type and the background.

The best solution is a black or dark gray background with a low percentage of black, which will appear almost white but will not "bloom" like a pure white.
The lighter the gray, the darker the type appears, even with the brightness of the type unchanged, because of the reduction in contrast. If the background is changed, then for the type to remain clearly legible, it too will need to be adjusted.
A combination of different grays creates a very calm image, but it is not recommended for longer texts because it is very low in contrast and can therefore be very tiring for the reader.

Black and gray background with gray type.

Color and Type
Color and Type

Background black 80 %,
Geneva black 50 %, 20 pt, 11 pt

Color and Type
Color and Type

Background black 70 %,
Geneva black 50 %, 20 pt, 11 pt

Color and Type
Color and Type

Background black 70 %,
Geneva black 40 %, 20 pt, 11 pt

Color and Type
Color and Type

Background black 50 %,
Geneva black 40 %, 20 pt, 11 pt

Color and Type
Color and Type

Background black 70 %,
Geneva black 100 %, 20 pt, 11 pt

Color and Type
Color and Type

Background black 60 %,
Geneva black 90 %, 20 pt, 11 pt

Color and Type
Color and Type

Background black 50 %,
Geneva black 80 %, 20 pt, 11 pt

Color and Type
Color and Type

Background black 100 %,
Geneva black 60 %, 20 pt, 11 pt

Color and Type
Color and Type

Background black 90 %,
Geneva black 60 %, 20 pt, 11 pt

chromatic and
achromatic contrasts

Color and Type
Color and Type

Background black 100%, Geneva red 100%

Color and Type
Color and Type

Background black 90%, Geneva red 100%

Color and Type
Color and Type

Background black 100%, Geneva green 100%

Color and Type
Color and Type

Background black 80%, Geneva green 100%

Color and Type
Color and Type

Background black 100%, Geneva blue 100%

Color and Type
Color and Type

Background black 70%, Geneva blue 100%

Primary colors of the additive color system on a black background

Primary colors of the additive color system on a gray background

Primary colors of the subtractive color system on a black background

Color and Type
Color and Type

Background black 100%,
Geneva magenta 100%

Color and Type
Color and Type

Background black 100%,
Geneva yellow 100%

Color and Type
Color and Type

Background black 100%,
Geneva cyan 100%

Because of the strong contrasts, typography using primary and secondary colors is not entirely suitable on a black background screen. The eyes will sense a flickering in these contrasts. Also as the eyes get tired, the text will begin to appear out of focus and it will require a great effort continually to bring the text into focus. But while these contrasts are not very suitable for body text, they can have an eye-catching effect and be useful to highlight individual words or headings.

Typography in primary or secondary colors on a gray background will appear less intense, but is still not advisable for longer texts.

Color and Type

Background black 100 %,
Geneva red 100 % and blue 100 %

Color and Type
Color and Type

Background black 100 %,
Geneva green 100 % and red 100 %

Primary colors of the subtractive color system on a gray background

Color and Type
Color and Type

Background black 90 %,
Geneva magenta 100 %

Color and Type
Color and Type

Background black 100 %,
Geneva blue 100 % and green 100 %

Color and Type
Color and Type

Background black 80 %,
Geneva yellow 100 %

Color and Type
Color and Type

Background black 70 %,
Geneva cyan 100 %

achromatic and chromatic contrasts

A good way of presenting typography as body text on a black background is to use tertiary colors which are lighter in tone. If the background is a dark gray, the colors of the type will appear less intensive. This is due to a reduction in contrast, which will improve legibility.

Conversely, if the gray is too light, or has the same intrinsic brightness, the text will be harder to read.
Similarly, type in a deep black or pure white on a chromatic background

Color and Type
Color and Type

Background black 70 %,
Geneva red 100 %, green 60 %, blue 40 %

Color and Type
Color and Type

Background black 100 %,
Geneva red 100 %, green 60 %, blue 40 %

Color and Type
Color and Type

Background black 90 %,
Geneva red 100 %, green 60 %, blue 40 %

Color and Type
Color and Type

Background black 100 %,
Geneva red 100 %, green 50 %, blue 50 %

Color and Type
Color and Type

Background black 90 %,
Geneva red 100 %, green 50 %, blue 50 %

Color and Type
Color and Type

Background black 100 %,
Geneva red 50 %, green 100 %, blue 50 %

Color and Type
Color and Type

Background black 90 %,
Geneva red 50 %, green 100 %, blue 50 %

Color and Type
Color and Type

Background black 100 %,
Geneva red 50 %, green 85 %, blue 50 %

Color and Type
Color and Type

Background black 90 %,
Geneva red 50 %, green 85 %, blue 100 %

often results in a contrast which is too strong. If a very dark or very light gray is used for the type, the reduction in contrast will be easier on the eyes. If black is mixed with primary colors which have a high color intensity, they appear less intense. The same applies to primary colors, which appear lighter when other primary colors are added to them.

The term "tertiary colors" is used for colors which result when a primary color is mixed with a secondary color or when two secondary colors are mixed together.

Color and Type
Color and Type

Background red 100 %,
Geneva black 100 %

Color and Type
Color and Type

Background green 100 %,
Geneva black 100 %

Color and Type
Color and Type

Background red 100 %,
Geneva black 90 %

Color and Type
Color and Type

Background green 100 %,
Geneva black 90 %

Color and Type
Color and Type

Background red 100 %, green 50 %, blue 50 %,
Geneva black 90 %

Color and Type
Color and Type

Background green 100 %, blue 33 %,
Geneva black 90 %

Color and Type
Color and Type

Background red 100 %,
Geneva white

Color and Type
Color and Type

Background green 100 %,
Geneva white

Color and Type
Color and Type

Background red 100 %,
Geneva black 15 %

Color and Type
Color and Type

Background green 100 %,
Geneva black 15 %

Color and Type
Color and Type

Background red 66 %, darkened with black,
Geneva black 15 %

Color and Type
Color and Type

Background green 50 %, darkened with black,
Geneva black 15 %

chromatic and achromatic contrasts

The choice of whether to use white or black type with a screen background color will depend on the intrinsic brightness of the type. If the difference in brightness between the background and the type is too small, the text will be hard to read. Yellow, for example, has a very high intrinsic brightness. If white and yellow are combined, therefore, there is not

Color and Type
Color and Type

Background blue 100%
Geneva black 100%

Color and Type
Color and Type

Background blue 100%
Geneva black 90%

Color and Type
Color and Type

Background red 50%, green 80%, blue 100%
Geneva black 90%

Color and Type
Color and Type

Background blue 100%
Geneva white

Color and Type
Color and Type

Background blue 100%
Geneva black 15%

Color and Type
Color and Type

Background blue 60%
darkened with black, Geneva black 15%

Color and Type
Color and Type

Background red 100%, green 100%
Geneva black 100%

Color and Type
Color and Type

Background red 100%, green 100%
Geneva black 90%

Color and Type
Color and Type

Background red 100%, green 100%, blue 70%
Geneva black 90%

Color and Type
Color and Type

Background red 100%, green 100%
Geneva white

Color and Type
Color and Type

Background red 100%, green 100%
Geneva black 15%

Color and Type
Color and Type

Background red 70%, green 70%
darkened with black, Geneva black 15%

enough difference in brightness between the two colors, making the text very hard to read. A combination of deep blue and black has a similar effect. Black has no intrinsic brightness, and blue has very little; if these two colors are combined, there is hardly any contrast. When gray type is used on a colored background, it is important to ensure that the gray

type shifts towards its complementary color, i.e. the color which is opposite it in the circle of color.
In short, dark chromatic colors make light or gray type appear more intense than chromatic colors with a medium brightness.

Background red 33 %, blue 100 %
Geneva black 100 %

Background red 33 %, blue 100 %
Geneva black 90 %

Background red 75 %, green 50 %, blue 100 %
Geneva black 90 %

Background red 33 %, blue 100 %
Geneva white

Background red 33 %, blue 100 %
Geneva black 20 %

Background red 10 %, blue 40 %
darkened with black, Geneva black 15 %

Background red 100 %, green 33 %
Geneva black 100 %

Background red 100 %, green 33 %
Geneva black 90 %

Background red 100 %, green 70 %, blue 50 %
Geneva black 90 %

Background red 100 %, green 33 %
Geneva white

Background red 100 %, green 33 %
Geneva black 20 %

Background red 85 %, blue 30 %
darkened with black, Geneva black 15 %

complementary contrasts

Complementary colors are colors which are opposite each other in the color circle. If these colors are combined as type and screen background, the result will be a flickering effect. Texts using these combinations are very difficult and tiring to read, especially on screen, where the color is made up of light.

Colors of the additive color system

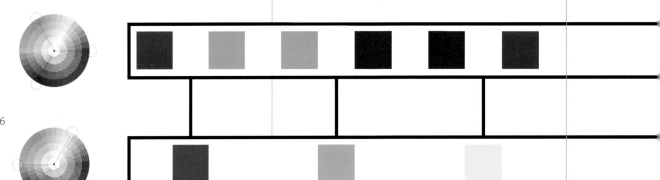

36

Colors of the subtractive color system

The color examples on this double page show the complementary contrasts of the primary colors with each of the colors from the additive color system (red, green, blue) compared with a color from the subtractive color system (cyan, yellow, magenta).

The series of contrasts was prepared with the RGB system.

Color and Type
Color and Type

Background green 100 %, blue 100 %
Geneva red 100 %, 20 pt, 11 pt

Color and Type
Color and Type

Background red 100 %
Geneva green 100 %, blue 100 %, 20 pt, 11 pt

Color and Type
Color and Type

Background red 100 %, blue 100 %
Geneva green 100 %, 20 pt, 11 pt

Color and Type
Color and Type

Background green 100 %
Geneva red 100 %, blue 100 %, 20 pt, 11 pt

Color and Type
Color and Type

Background red 100 %, green 100 %
Geneva blue 100 %, 20 pt, 11 pt

Color and Type
Color and Type

Background blue 100 %,
Geneva red 100 %, green 100 %, 20 pt, 11 pt

complementary contrasts

The series of complementary color contrasts also includes the achromatic contrast of black and white.

Taking the progression of complementary contrasts starting from the primary colors as the basis of a combination of type and background, some of the intermediate stages are quite easy to read. These intermediate stages are combinations which contain no primary colors. The purer a color is, the more sparingly it should be used. Contrasts in which the background color has little intrinsic brightness or intensity are more easily legible than combinations in which the background color has a high intrinsic brightness.

Color and Type
Color and Type

Background black,
Geneva white, 20 pt, 11 pt

Color and Type
Color and Type

Background white,
Geneva black, 20 pt, 11 pt

Colors of the subtractive color system

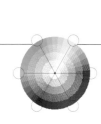

Colors of the additive color system

Blue, for example, has a relatively low intrinsic brightness and is therefore quite legible even with its complementary color.

Color and Type
Color and Type

Background green 100 %,
Geneva red 100 %, blue 100 %, 20 pt, 11 pt

Color and Type
Color and Type

Background green 100 %, blue 33 %
Geneva red 100%, blue 66 %, 20 pt, 11 pt

Color and Type
Color and Type

Background green 100 %, blue 66 %
Geneva red 100%, blue 33 %, 20 pt, 11 pt

Color and Type
Color and Type

Background green 100 %, blue 100 %
Geneva red 100%, 20 pt, 11 pt

Color and Type
Color and Type

Background green 66 %, blue 100 %
Geneva red 100%, green 33 %, 20 pt, 11 pt

Color and Type
Color and Type

Background green 33 %, blue 100 %
Geneva red 100%, green 66 %, 20 pt, 11 pt

Color and Type
Color and Type

Background, blue 100 %
Geneva red 100%, green 100 %, 20 pt, 11 pt

"Warmer" colors are less suitable as a background in terms of good legibility than "cold" background colors. Smaller type is especially difficult to read because of the strong flickering effect. An exception is the fifth example on the right (orange/blue).

If the color of the type is made darker or brighter, depending on the brightness of the background, it is then possible to achieve quite reasonable results.

Color and Type
Color and Type

Background red 33 %, blue 100 %
Geneva red 66 %, green 100 %, 20 pt, 11 pt

Color and Type
Color and Type

Background red 33 %, blue 100 %
Geneva greatly brightened, 20 pt, 11 pt

Color and Type
Color and Type

Background red 66 %, blue 100 %
Geneva red 33 %, green 100 %, 20 pt, 11 pt

Color and Type
Color and Type

Background red 100 %, blue 100 %
Geneva green 100 %, 20 pt, 11 pt

Color and Type
Color and Type

Background red 100 %, blue 66 %,
Geneva green 100 %, blue 33 %, 20 pt, 11 pt

Color and Type
Color and Type

Background red 100 %, blue 33 %
Geneva green 100%, blue 66 %, 20 pt, 11 pt

Color and Type
Color and Type

Background red 100 %, blue 33 %
Geneva strongly darkened, 20 pt, 11 pt

Color and Type
Color and Type

Background red 100 %
Geneva green 100 %, blue 100 %, 20 pt, 11 pt

Color and Type
Color and Type

Background red 100 %, green 33 %
Geneva green 66 %, blue 100 %, 20 pt, 11 pt

Color and Type
Color and Type

Background red 100 %, green 66 %
Geneva green 33 %, blue 100 %, 20 pt, 11 pt

Color and Type
Color and Type

Background red 100 %, green 100 %
Geneva blue 100 %, 20 pt, 11 pt

contrasting brightness

If type and screen backgrounds using colors with the same intrinsic brightness are combined, the text will be hard to read. Without contrasts, the text and background become an indistinct haze. This is particularly the case with very light or very dark colors with a similar intrinsic brightness. An added problem with very light color combinations of the same intrinsic brightness is the effect of "blooming" as a result of the light.

The situation is similar for colors which are close together in the color circle, such as red and orange.

If related colors with insufficient contrast in brightness are combined, the legibility of the text will be further reduced.

It is therefore best to combine colors which have a different intrinsic brightness. The contrast should not be too strong, on the other hand, or legibility will be impaired by flickering. In particular, where dark type appears on a bright background, the type may be "bloomed out" by the brightness of the background, quite apart from the fact that very bright colors are intrinsically unsuitable as a screen background.

Color and Type
Color and Type

Background white, Geneva yellow

Color and Type
Color and Type

Background yellow, Geneva white

Color and Type
Color and Type

Background yellow, Geneva orange

Color and Type
Color and Type

Background orange, Geneva yellow

Color and Type
Color and Type

Background orange, Geneva red

Color and Type
Color and Type

Background orange, Geneva green

Color and Type
Color and Type

Background orange, Geneva grey

Color and Type
Color and Type

Background red, Geneva orange

Background red, Geneva violet

Color and Type
Color and Type

Background green, Geneva orange

Color and Type
Color and Type

Background green, Geneva violet

Color and Type
Color and Type

Background gray, Geneva orange

Color and Type
Color and Type

Background gray, Geneva violet

Color and Type
Color and Type

Background orange, Geneva gray

Background violet, Geneva blue

Background violet, Geneva red

Color and Type
Color and Type

Background violet, Geneva green

Background violet, Geneva gray

Background blue, Geneva black

Color and Type
Color and Type

Background blue, Geneva violet

Background black, Geneva blue

Color and Type
Color and Type

Background blue, Geneva light violet

color combinations

To produce attractive color combinations, it is possible to use contrasts which combine the colors of other color relationships. For example, cold or warm colors can be combined with each other.
More striking is a contrast of warm and cold, or a contrast in which the respective complementary color is loosely related to the colors used.

The color circle can be used here as a guide to help define the complementary contrast of a particular color. When the complementary color has been found, colors which are broadly related to this color can be selected from the color circle. Another way of combining colors successfully is to contrast dark with light.

Warm-cold contrasts

Color and Type
Color and Type

Background red 100 %, green 66 %
Geneva green 33%, blue 100%, 20 pt, 11 pt

Color and Type
Color and Type

Background red 100 %
Geneva red 50 %, green 80 %, blue 100 %, 20 pt, 11 pt

Color and Type
Color and Type

Background green 100 %, blue 33 %
Geneva red 100 %, green 33 %, 20 pt, 11 pt

Color and Type
Color and Type

Background green 33 %, blue 100 %
Geneva red 100 %, green 85 %, blue 45 %, 20 pt, 11 pt

Warm-warm contrasts

Color and Type
Color and Type

Background red 100 %
Geneva red 100 %, green 66 %, 20 pt, 11 pt

Color and Type
Color and Type

Background red 100 %, green 33 %
Geneva red 100 %, green 100 %, 20 pt, 11 pt

Color and Type
Color and Type

Background red 100 %, green 100 %
Geneva red 100 %, blue 66 %, 20 pt, 11 pt

Cold-cold contrasts

Color and Type
Color and Type

Background blue 100 %
Geneva green 100 %, blue 33 %, 20 pt, 11 pt

Color and Type
Color and Type

Background red 33 %, blue 100 %
Geneva green 100 %, blue 100 %, 20 pt, 11 pt

Color and Type
Color and Type

Background green 100 %, blue 66 %
Geneva blue 100 %, 20 pt, 11 pt

With the contrasts mentioned, "blooming" and possible flickering effects must be avoided. This danger particularly applies to colors which have a high intrinsic brightness or which are complementarily opposite each other in the color circle.
If a colored type is combined with a colored background, it is essential to increase the tracking of the type.

Colors related to the complementary colors

Color and Type
Color and Type

Background red 100 %
Geneva green 100 %, blue 66 % brightened with 60 %, 20 pt, 11 pt

Color and Type
Color and Type

Background green 100 %, blue 33 %
Geneva red 66 %, blue 100 % brightened with 80 %, 20 pt, 11 pt

Color and Type
Color and Type

Background red 66 %, blue 100 %
Geneva green 100 %, blue 100 % brightened with 80 %, 20 pt, 11 pt

Color and Type
Color and Type

Background green 33 %, blue 100 %
Geneva red 66 %, green 100 %, 20 pt, 11 pt

Color and Type
Color and Type

Background red 100 %, green 100 %
Geneva green 66 %, blue 100 %, 20 pt, 11 pt

45

light and dark contrasts

A dark-colored background contrasted with a light type color is very comfortable for the eyes for long sessions at the computer screen. The darker the screen, i.e. the more "dead light" meets the eye, the better it is for the viewer because over-stimulation and the resulting loss of concentration can largely be eliminated.
However, the matching lighter color of type must be selected very carefully to avoid "blooming".

On the other hand, color combinations which are too balanced and have a calm, dark background run the risk of losing their visual attraction. The designer can get around this by, for example, reversing the colors on pages which will not be looked at for long periods, such as title pages, pages without much text, etc: the type will then use the color normally used for the background, and vice versa.
It is also possible to change the background colors to other dark colors, for example, in order to distinguish the chapters from each other. Or the type color can be changed while keeping the background the same. This will help the reader find his or her way around the text.
 A further possibility, for pages which will only be looked at briefly, is to display the type in the same type color as the background in a different intensity so that the type will be legible.

Contrasting tones can be used as background aids to identification and orientation or a pattern of different tones can help bring a dark background to life.

Color and Type
Color and Type

Color and Type
Color and Type

Color and Type
Color and Type

Color and Type
Color and Type

Color and Type
Color and Type

Background red 30 %

Color and Type
Color and Type

Background white
Geneva red 30 %, 20 pt, 11 pt

Color and Type
Color and Type

Color and Type
Color and Type

Color and Type
Color and Type

Color and Type
Color and Type

Color and Type
Color and Type

Color and Type
Color and Type

Background red 25%, blue 25%

Color and Type
Color and Type

Color and Type
Color and Type

Color and Type
Color and Type

Color and Type
Color and Type

Color and Type
Color and Type

Background blue 30%

light and dark contrasts

Color and Type
Color and Type

Color and Type
Color and Type

Color and Type
Color and Type

Color and Type
Color and Type

Color and Type
Color and Type

Color and Type
Color and Type

Color and Type
Color and Type

Color and Type
Color and Type

Color and Type
Color and Type

Color and Type
Color and Type

Background green 25%, blue 25%

Background green 100%

Color and Type
Color and Type

Color and Type
Color and Type

Color and Type
Color and Type

Color and Type
Color and Type

Color and Type
Color and Type

Background red 25 %, blue 25 %

Yellow is only occasionally suitable as a dark background because of its high intrinsic brightness. When darkened, it will always look dirty.

Color and Type
Color and Type

Background red 60 %, green 40 %

combinations of color tones

Color and Type
Color and **Type**

Background red 2%, green 6%, blue 41%
Univers red 2%, green 6%, blue 41%,
brightened with 40%

Color and Type
Color and Type

Background black 100%
Univers black 85%, 20 pt
Univers black 80%, 11 pt

Color and Type
Color and **Type**

Background red 100%
Univers red 85%, 20 pt
Univers red 70%, 11 pt

Color and Type
Color and Type

Background red 66%
Univers red 66%, 20 pt brightened with 80%
Univers red 66%, 11 pt brightened with 70%

Color and Type
Color and **Type**

Background green 50%
Univers green 50%, 20 pt brightened with 70%
Univers green 50%, 11 pt brightened with 65%

Color and Type
Color and Type

Background yellow 100%
Univers yellow 100%, green 66%, 20 pt brightened with 80%
Univers yellow 100%, green 66%, 11 pt brightened with 70%

Combinations of different tones of the same color are too monotonous for use as reading texts.
At first glance they look attractive, but they are tiring and lack tension and contrast. If the tone of the background and type are adapted to each other, combinations of different tones of the same color can be used as an attractive screen background, creating identity and a strong visual impression for logos, company names, or the heading of a particular page.

It is a basic principle that the smaller and thinner the type, the darker it will appear. The larger and bolder the type, the lighter it will appear. This difference can be compensated for – or it can be made use of:
If the color tones vary, the screen background acquires a spatial dimension; light-colored type appears nearer, dark type appears further away. This makes the overall impression more dynamic. If dark backgrounds are used, the screen background appears lighter without the eyes being irritated by too much brightness. If a background is selected with a color of a high intrinsic brightness, such as yellow, the tone variations of the type will need to be darker to make the overall impression calmer.

lor and nd Typ

Color and Type

51

Color and Type

Background yellow 100 %
Univers in different sizes, brightened or darkened

Color and Type

Background dark blue
Univers in different sizes, brightened to different extents

ergonomic design of
the computer workplace

The ideal distance between the eyes and the computer screen is 46 to 56cm. However, the eyes can adapt to a viewing distance of between 33cm and 74cm. The size and brightness of the screen obviously need to be taken into consideration. The viewing angle should not be more than 30 degrees.

The illustration shows a seating position which enables the person to work comfortably. However, this does not mean that sitting with a straight back and a right-angled arm and leg position is the only "right" position throughout the day.
Ideally, the posture should be changed from time to time to remain mobile.

A sensible level for the working surface (desk height) is between 68cm and 76cm. The standard desk has a working height of 72 cm, which, combined with a keyboard height of 3cm, provides a working height of 75cm. Given this desk height, the chair, ergonomically speaking, should be adjustable between a height of 42 and 52cm.

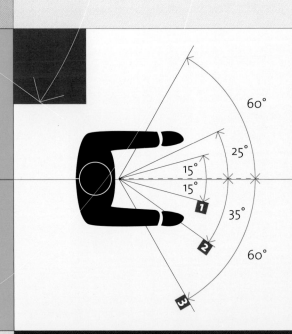

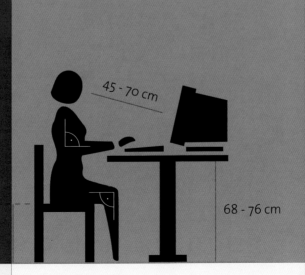

3

2

1

45°

35°

15°

15°

25°

35°

1 Ideal viewing area

2 Maximum viewing area without moving the head

3 Extended viewing area with movement of the head

53

45 - 70 cm

68 - 76 cm

42 - 52 cm

3

TYPOGRAPHY AND

LEGIBILITY
ON PAPER

Serifs are small strokes added to the ends of the letters.

Times
with serifs

56

Univers
without serifs

There are two basic forms of typeface in modern typography: **antique** or **serif**, and **grotesque** or **sans serif**.

Antique typefaces have clearly emphasized serifs and clear differences in the thickness of the strokes that make up the letter. These typefaces are most often used for text in books and newspapers.

Grotesque typefaces are faces without serifs, and they have no differences, or only slight differences, in the thickness of the strokes. These typefaces are most often used for titles, headings, and in advertising.

At the normal type size, antique typefaces are less suitable for use on the screen than grotesque typefaces.
If antique typefaces are being used on the screen, it is important to select a typeface in which the serifs and strokes are not too thin.

Antiqua
Times

Grotesque
Univers

typefaces

■

Antique typefaces

Baskerville
Bodoni
Bookman
Caslon
Clarendon
Garamond
Goudy
Joanna
Lucida
New York
Palatino
Poppl-Pontifex
Sabon
Times
Walbaum
Weidemann

Grotesque typefaces

Avant Garde
Avenir
Akzidenz Grotesk
Chicago
Frutiger
Futura
Geneva
Gill
Helvetica
News Gothic
Quay
Syntax
Univers

Avant Garde

Bodoni

Chicago

Clarendon

Frutiger

Garamond

Geneva

Joanna

Helvetica

Palatino

Syntax

Times

Univers

Univers

thin

normal

semi-bold

bold

italic

narrow

broad

color

underlined

s p a c e d

CAPITALS

grotesque face

antique face

SMALL CAPITALS

To highlight passages in a text with a uniform type size, the designer has several options. He or she can highlight text by using thin, semi-bold, bold, and italic styles, underlining, spacing, narrow and broad type, small capitals and capitals, or switch between sans serif and serif typefaces.
Colors can, of course, also be used as a form of highlighting.

A further option is a change of type size, although this should be used sparingly to avoid creating a restless typographical impression.

Each typeface has its own mood, which can be emphasized by the use of italic type, narrow spacing, wide spacing, bold or semi-bold type.

The possibilities are endless, but it is advisable not to use these features for ordinary body text. They are most effective when restricted to single words (e.g. in posters), logos, and headlines.

Bricklayer Times, italic

JEWELLER Helvetica

BRICKLAYER

Jeweler

fast Helvetica

s l o w

full

empty

Type size

interlinear spacing

Text
without
interlinear spacing

Text overlapping
one line below
the next

Text

with extra

interlinear spacing

Text
with normal
interlinear spacing

Interlinear spacing is an important criterion in deciding whether the reader will physically enjoy reading a text.

The interlinear spacing, measured from the base line of the type to the mean line of the following line, should be at least one and a half times the x height.

For long lines, more generous interlinear spacing should be used than for short lines, to enable the eye to jump more easily to the next line.

If the interlinear spacing is too large, the reader is aware not only of the lines themselves, but also the gaps between them. The result is a structure of positive and negative elements which may irritate the eyes. Instead, the interlinear spacing should be selected so that the reader concentrates on the lines, not the spaces in between.

59

Cap line

x height

Descender

Ascender

Typeface

Base line of type

type sizes

DTP point = 0.352 mm

Most DTP programs use the measurement system of the DTP point, which is abbreviated as "pt". Other systems, such as the Didot point (0.375 mm) are increasingly being pushed into the background by computer-assisted design.

Type size is of fundamental importance for legibility.

Text that is printed smaller than 6pt is hardly legible.

When the type size is measured with a typometer, the capital letter must fit exactly between the horizontal lines (the best letters for the purpose are E, H, and M).
To double-check, it is advisable to compare with the sizes above and below the type size measured.
In reading texts, a minimum type size of 8 to 10pt is advisable.
Sub-headings should be between 12 and 14pt, and headings should be set in 14 to 18pt.

The type size is dependent on the format in which the text is planned to appear, the column width, and the quantity of text.

Texts which will need to be transmitted by fax should not contain type that is smaller than 10pt. This is an important consideration in the design of logos and addresses, which usually need to be suitable for fax transmission.

Univers 6 pt   Univers 9 pt   Univers 12 pt   Univers 14 pt   Univers 18 pt

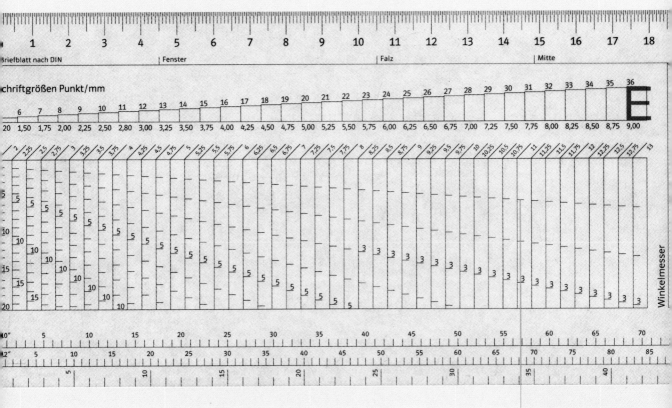

| 1 | 2 | 3 | 4 | 5 | 6 | 7 | 8 | 9 | 10 | 11 | 12 | 13 | 14 | 15 | 16 | 17 | 18 |

Briefblatt nach DIN · Fenster · Falz · Mitte

Schriftgrößen Punkt/mm

36 35 34 33 32 31 30 29 28 27 26 25 24 23 22 21 20 19 18 17 16 15 14 13 12 11 10 9 8 7 6

9,00 8,75 8,50 8,25 8,00 7,75 7,50 7,25 7,00 6,75 6,50 6,25 6,00 5,75 5,50 5,25 5,00 4,75 4,50 4,25 4,00 3,75 3,50 3,25 3,00 2,80 2,50 2,25 2,00 1,75 1,50 20

Winkelmesser

Scales to determine the interlinear spacing. The base lines should be placed against these lines.

nivers 24 pt   Univers 36 pt   Unive

text layout

This is an example of a text which has more than fifty letters in each line. The extra interlinear

spacing helps the reader's eyes to jump from the end of the line to the beginning of the next.

A normal line has a length of about fifty letters. For lines of this length "automatic" interlinear spacing can be used when working with the computer.

Long lines with more than fifty letters need extra interlinear spacing to help the eyes to find the beginning of the next line more easily.

Short lines can manage without any extra interlinear spacing if the text is not too long.

Even if the text is clearly structured, it may be difficult to read it if the lines are too short. But where there is only a small amount of text, as in picture captions and notes, short lines are perfectly legible.

Even if the text is clearly structured, it may be difficult to read it if the lines are too short. But where there is only a small amount of text, as in picture captions and notes, short lines are perfectly legible.

This is an example of a short text with less than fifty letters in each line and with narrow interlinear spacing.

A text with short lines can be set in smaller type than a text with longer lines. But small type should only be used for short texts, which means that the body type, i.e., the main text, should be set in a suitable size. When reading a text, the eyes are very sensitive to interference, even if it only consists of small details, such as letters that are too close together.

type alignment

■

This short text is
centered, i.e., the lines are aligned
around a central axis. There
is no straight edge
at the beginning and end
of the lines.

Univers 55

This short text is aligned to the
left and ragged on the right,
i.e., the left edge is straight,
whereas the line lengths on the
right vary.

This text is justified to the left but
only moderately ragged to the
right because it uses hyphena-
tion. This avoids the disadvantages of justified text (oversize
word spacing, "holes"), but it
makes good use of the space.

This short text is aligned to the
right and ragged on the left,
i.e., the lines are flush with the
right edge and vary in their
length on the left.

This short text is fully justified,
i.e., the beginnings and ends of
the line form a straight edge on
both left and right. This is
achieved by varying the gaps
between the words.

The alignment of the type
determines the typographical
appearance of a text. There is a
huge difference between justified
text which uses the entire
column width (e.g. in
newspapers), centered text (e.g.
in invitations), and text that is
justified to the right or left only.
Right justified text or centered
text is only suitable for small
amounts of text because the eye
does not immediately find the
beginning of the next line.
(This applies only to western
languages, which are read from
left to right.)
Text with ragged edges, which
seems to be in fashion at the
moment, often gives the text a
restless appearance.

word spacing

In fully justified text, as here, it is unavoidable that the spaces between the words are of different sizes, because all the lines are of the same length. To avoid this, with justified text, the columns should not be too narrow.

When setting a text, excessive concentrations of black type and over-sized white "holes" should be avoided to ensure that the text is easy to read. The spacing between individual words must always be seen in relation to the letter spacing and tracking, so that the individual word can still be identified as a word. If the tracking is increased, the word spacing must also be increased.

As a general rule, it is usually sufficient if the spacing between words in body text is equal to the width of a small "i".

Another rule: narrow and bold styles have smaller internal spacing within the letters (counters), and they can therefore be set with smaller spacing between letters and words.

Broad and thin styles, on the other hand, have larger spaces within the letters (counters), and should therefore be set with larger spacing between letters and words.

This is an example of a text which has excessive concentrations of black type and white holes. This is obviously uncomfortable for the reader. In fully justified text like this paragraph, differences in the spacing between words are unavoidable because all of the lines are equal in length. Again, it is important to ensure that the column width for justified text is not too narrow.

If the tracking...

If the tracking...

The body width of the small i regulates the word spacing.

An example of different word spacing
Helvetica, Compressed 16°

An example of different word spacing
Helvetica, bold 16°

An example of different word spacing
Helvetica, extended 16°

An example of different word spacing
Helvetica, light 16°

An example of different word spacing
Avant Garde, 16°

a Helvetica 16°, Ultra Compressed

a Helvetica 16°, bold

a Helvetica 16°

a Avant Garde, 16°

The "counter" width varies, depending on the style and the type family.

VᴀsᴇE

VASE

V

Width to right (kern)

A

Width to left

66

E

Balanced typography not only depends on balanced word spacing, it also involves balanced letter spacing within the words. If the letter spacing is too narrow or too wide, the text will be hard to read. If the spacing is too narrow, the individual letters may merge together so that it is difficult to distinguish them from each other. If the letter spacing is too wide, the reader will perceive a gap, and there is a risk that individual words will seem to break up into an incoherent series of letters. It is therefore advisable not to select wide letter spacing for long texts.

Small type needs wider letter spacing than large type. When the type size is increased, this does not mean that the letter spacing can be enlarged by the same amount.

A, L, T, V, and W are capital letters which create large gaps. The same applies to the small f, r, v, and y. That means that the spacing to the following letter should be reduced by kerning. When deciding whether kerning is advisable or not, the left and right width of each individual letter must be considered.

Typefaces that are used on a computer have kerning tables already integrated in the software which contain values that are acceptable for use on paper. It is therefore only worthwhile to change individual letter spacing values for very large type sizes, especially as this is a very time-consuming process.

If the letter spacing is too narrow, the individual letters may run into each other.

If the letter spacing is too wide, the words seem to break up.

Small type needs wider letter spacing than large type.

Small type needs wider letter spacing than large type.

definitions

Antique face	Typeface with serifs
Ascender	The part of lower case letters which projects above the x height
Bitmap type	Typeface made up of pixels
Body type	Main typefaces used for body text in books and newspapers; all typefaces except headings and marginal notes
Body width	Overall width of a letter
Cap line	Height of capital letters, »H«
Centered type	Text aligned around a central axis
Counter	Space within letters, e.g. in an »O«
Didot point	Measurement unit for type size (0.375 mm / abbreviation: dd)
DTP point	Measurement unit for type size (0.352 mm / abbreviation: pt)
Egyptienne	A serif typeface without hairlines, but with bold down strokes
Fraktur	Gothic type
Fully justified text	Text with lines that cover the full column width
Grotesque face	Sans serif typeface, typeface without serifs
Gutter	(US) Distance between columns
Interlinear spacing	Space between one line and the next
Kerning	Reduced spacing between letters
Left justified	Text with a straight left edge, follows the normal reading flow
Legibility	Criteria: interlinear spacing, type size, tracking, line length
Line length	Column width
Majuscule	Upper case letter, capital letter
Marginal notes	Notes in the margin
Minuscule	Lower case letter, small letter
Modified ragged	Ragged typesetting with hyphenation
Pictogram	Visual symbol that can be understood in any language
Ragged text	Typesetting with varying line-lengths
Right justified	Text with a straight right edge and a ragged left edge, goes against the flow of reading in western cultures
Sans serif	Typeface without serifs
Small caps	Letters which have the height of an »x« and the shape of a capital
Style	Bold, semi-bold, normal, light, italic
Tracking	Spacing between the letters
Upper case	Capital letters
Wide spacing	Increased spacing between letters
Word spacing	Space between the individual words (quad)

TYPOGRAPHY AND

4

LEGIBILITY
ON THE SCREEN

typefaces and
suitability for the screen

Text on the screen is tiring to read, and so long passages of unbroken text should be avoided. The tight and full text layout found in magazines is used partly for economic reasons.

In screen design, however, this cost factor is hardly relevant. For this reason and to encourage the reader to continue, texts on screen should be designed generously and with wide interlinear spacing.

But, on the other hand, the user can also find frequent "scrolling" in a document tiring if the text is distributed over several pages.

In some cases, there is a matching bitmap for a specific typeface and a specific size, but the word and line spacing still need to be checked and corrected accordingly. This is particularly important since reading on the screen can be difficult for those who are not accustomed to it.

Displaying type on the screen requires a high degree of compromise.

This is because screen display at present is based on a bitmap of 72 pixels (dots) per inch. This resolution requires special processing for small type sizes up to about 20pt, depending on the bitmap. Without this processing, distortion occurs in the bitmap.

As conventional typefaces cannot be simply transferred to the screen, there are special screen typefaces such as Chicago, Geneva, Monaco, and New York. Their type design is specially adapted to the bitmap of a 72 dpi screen and optimized for reading.

Monaco

abcdefghijklmnopqrstuvwxyz
ABCDEFGHIJKLMNOPQRSTUVWXYZ
1234567890

Chicago

Color and Type

abcdefghijklmnopqrstuvwxyz
ABCDEFGHIJKLMNOPQRSTUVWXYZ
1234567890

71

Color and Type

Geneva

abcdefghijklmnopqrstuvwxyz
ABCDEFGHIJKLMNOPQRSTUVWXYZ
1234567890

New York

Color and Type

abcdefghijklmnopqrstuvwxyz
ABCDEFGHIJKLMNOPQRSTUVWXYZ
1234567890

typefaces and
suitability for the screen

Typefaces such as OCR A and the optimized form, OCR B, are typefaces which were specially developed as computer-readable typefaces (OCR = optical character recognition). OCR A is very clear, if rather stilted. This is because it was designed for early computers, which, by modern standards, had a very limited text recognition capacity.

Looking closely at the individual letters of OCR A, it is noticeable that an effort has been made to avoid round and oblique forms, which are difficult to display on the screen. For example, a small "o" looks almost like a small square with rounded corners, a capital "W" does not have the characteristic oblique strokes, and in the capital "V" the ends are vertical strokes.

Color and Type   OCR A

ABCDEFGHIJKLMNOPQRSTUVWXYZ
abcdefghijklmnopqrstuvwxyz
1234567890

Color and Type   OCR A

Color and Type   OCR B

Color and Type   Chicago

Color and Type   Helvetica

A comparison with other typefaces shows that OCR A has a very wide tracking value and does not always take optimum character equalization into account. As a result of these special characteristics, this typeface has been used not only on the screen over recent years, but has also influenced trends in typography on paper.

Color and Type

A B C D E F G H I J K L M N O P Q R S T U V W X Y Z
a b c d e f g h i j k l m n o p q r s t u v w x y z
1 2 3 4 5 6 7 8 9 0

o W V   OCR A

o W V   Helvetica

pixels and bitmaps

A "dot" is the smallest item which can be displayed on a computer screen; the next smallest item is a "pixel". The word is an abbreviation of "picture" and "element" and represents the smallest point in a picture.

A "pixel" can assume different brightness and intensity levels of a basic color. The possible brightness levels are determined by the number of dots per pixel. A (binary) choice is made as to whether a dot should light up or not. A matrix grid made up, for example, of 16 x 16 individual spaces into which the black dots can be inserted gives rise to 256 shades of gray. The term "bitmap" is made up from the words "bit" (= binary digit) and "map".

One bit corresponds to a black or white pixel, so a bitmap is a »map« of the "bits". A bitmap shows where each individual pixel is positioned in a specific type size, for example in order to display a typeface on the screen in a specific type size or a specific style. A pixel can be part of a text, line, or picture. The screen surface can be thought of as a collection of pixels which are in positions defined in terms of rows and columns.

When a typeface is chosen, a decision is effectively made as to which rows and columns should be used to display a typeface or picture made up of pixels. Because of their modular character, pixels can be used to portray almost anything, but they have the disadvantage of being governed by a grid structure. This is particularly noticeable in small type sizes.

Bitmap
1 bit $\hat{=}$ 1 pixel (black square)
Map $\hat{=}$ map of pixels

dpi $\hat{=}$ dots per inch
1 inch $\hat{=}$ 25, 4 mm
1 pixel $\hat{=}$ 1/72 inch (0,353 mm)
12 pixel $\hat{=}$ 1 pica (4,236 mm)
1 inch $\hat{=}$ 6 picas

9, 12, 18, 24 and 36 pt

9 pt	10 pt	12 pt	14 pt	16 pt

18 pt	20 pt	24 pt	36 pt

The type sizes shown do not correspond to the original type sizes.

Resolution and depth of color of the monitor

1 bit	$\stackrel{\wedge}{=}$	black & white	$\stackrel{\wedge}{=}$ $2^1 \stackrel{\wedge}{=} 2$	$\stackrel{\wedge}{=}$ 0 (0 or 1 corresponds to white or black)
2 bits	$\stackrel{\wedge}{=}$	4 shades of gray	$\stackrel{\wedge}{=}$ $2^2 \stackrel{\wedge}{=} 4$	$\stackrel{\wedge}{=}$ 01 (00 = white: 01 = light gray; 10 = dark gray; 11 = black)
2 bits	$\stackrel{\wedge}{=}$	4 colors	$\stackrel{\wedge}{=}$ $2^2 \stackrel{\wedge}{=} 4$	$\stackrel{\wedge}{=}$ 01
4 bits	$\stackrel{\wedge}{=}$	16 shades of gray	$\stackrel{\wedge}{=}$ $2^4 \stackrel{\wedge}{=} 16$	$\stackrel{\wedge}{=}$ 0101
4 bits	$\stackrel{\wedge}{=}$	16 colors	$\stackrel{\wedge}{=}$ $2^4 \stackrel{\wedge}{=} 16$	$\stackrel{\wedge}{=}$ 0101
8 bits	$\stackrel{\wedge}{=}$	256 shades of gray	$\stackrel{\wedge}{=}$ $2^8 \stackrel{\wedge}{=} 256$	$\stackrel{\wedge}{=}$ 01010101
8 bits	$\stackrel{\wedge}{=}$	256 colors	$\stackrel{\wedge}{=}$ $2^8 \stackrel{\wedge}{=} 256$	$\stackrel{\wedge}{=}$ 01010101
16 bits	$\stackrel{\wedge}{=}$	32,000 colors	$\stackrel{\wedge}{=}$ $2^{16} \stackrel{\wedge}{=} 32.768$	$\stackrel{\wedge}{=}$ 0101010101010101
24 bits	$\stackrel{\wedge}{=}$	1.6 Mio. colors	$\stackrel{\wedge}{=}$ $2^{24} \stackrel{\wedge}{=} 16.777.216$	$\stackrel{\wedge}{=}$ 010101010101010101010101

standard typefaces

A comparison with Futura shows that Univers has a much better appearance at 14 pt.

Before using a "standard" typeface on the computer screen, it is advisable to study the bitmap of the typeface at different sizes.

When studying the bitmaps of a typeface it is particularly important to check those letters which have round forms (such as the "o") and oblique strokes (such as the "w").
This will make it possible to decide quickly whether a typeface is suitable for use at a particular size.
It is not only the pixels that need to be studied – the letter spacing should also be inspected. If the letters are too close together, the text will be difficult to read because the letters clump together, even if the pixel pattern of the letters is acceptable.
In this case, the typeface should be rejected or the tracking value adjusted.

The example of Univers shows that it is perfectly possible to use "standard" typefaces on the screen without too much loss of legibility. But if small type is wanted on the screen, the standard typefaces are not usually suitable. As an alternative, Geneva is very suitable for use at 9 pt. This typeface was developed particularly for the computer screen, even for use with smaller type sizes. Apple Macintosh users will be familiar with Geneva at this size because it is the typeface used for the names of folders etc., on the desktop.

FUTURA

Fwogm	9 pt	Fwogm	**Geneva 9 pt**
	10 pt	Fwogm	
	11 pt	Fwogm	
	12 pt	Fwogm	
	13 pt	Fwogm	
Fwogm	14 pt	Fwogm	**Univers 14 pt**
	15 pt	Fwogm	
	16 pt	Fwogm	
	17 pt	Fwogm	
	18 pt	Fwogm	
	19 pt	Fwogm	
	20 pt	Fwogm	
	21 pt	Fwogm	
	22 pt	Fwogm	
	23 pt	Fwogm	
	24 pt	Fwogm	

Fwogm

UNIVERS

GENEVA

The bitmap of Geneva from 9 – 24 pt. It can clearly be seen that these bitmaps are more balanced than those for Univers 55.

The bitmap of Univers 55 from 9 – 24 pt. It can clearly be seen that the bitmap is only balanced at 14 pt.

Univers is perfectly suitable for use on the screen if it is displayed at 14 pt. A type size of 14 pt is also a pleasant size for reading texts on the screen.

pt	GENEVA	UNIVERS
9 pt	Fwogm	Fwogm
10 pt	Fwogm	Fwogm
11 pt	Fwogm	Fwogm
12 pt	Fwogm	Fwogm
13 pt	Fwogm	Fwogm
14 pt	Fwogm	Fwogm
15 pt	Fwogm	Fwogm
16 pt	Fwogm	Fwogm
17 pt	Fwogm	Fwogm
18 pt	Fwogm	Fwogm
19 pt	Fwogm	Fwogm
20 pt	Fwogm	Fwogm
21 pt	Fwogm	Fwogm
22 pt	Fwogm	Fwogm
23 pt	Fwogm	Fwogm
24 pt	Fwogm	Fwogm

The bitmap
of Geneva
from 9 – 24 pt.
These bitmaps are
clearly more
balanced than
those for Frutiger,
especially at very
small type sizes.

	GENEVA	FRUTIGER
9 pt	Fwogm	Fwogm
10 pt	Fwogm	Fwogm
11 pt	Fwogm	Fwogm
12 pt	Fwogm	Fwogm
13 pt	Fwogm	Fwogm
14 pt	Fwogm	Fwogm
15 pt	Fwogm	Fwogm
16 pt	Fwogm	**Fwogm**
17 pt	Fwogm	**Fwogm**
18 pt	Fwogm	**Fwogm**
19 pt	Fwogm	Fwogm
20 pt	Fwogm	Fwogm
21 pt	Fwogm	Fwogm
22 pt	Fwogm	Fwogm
23 pt	Fwogm	Fwogm
24 pt	Fwogm	Fwogm

The bitmap of
Frutiger from
9 – 24 pt.
The bitmap only
appears balanced
at 14 and 15 pt
and larger.

At certain type
sizes, Frutiger is
very suitable as a
Standard typeface
for display on the
computer screen.

78

comparison of
geneva, courier, and gill sans

Some of the Standard typefaces are perfectly suitable for use in text on the screen, with the restriction that they should be used at specific sizes which need to be determined individually.

The bitmap of Geneva from 9 – 24 pt. The bitmaps are clearly more balanced than those for Courier and Gill Sans, especially at very small type sizes.

The bitmap of Courier from 9 – 24 pt. The bitmap is only balanced at 14 and 17 pt.

The bitmap of Gill Sans from 9 – 24 pt. The bitmap is only balanced at 16 and 17 pt.

GENEVA	COURIER	GILL SANS
9 pt Fwogm	9 pt Fwgom	9 pt Fwgom
10 pt Fwogm	10 pt Fwgom	10 pt Fwgom
11 pt Fwogm	11 pt Fwgom	11 pt Fwgom
12 pt Fwogm	12 pt Fwgom	12 pt Fwgom
13 pt Fwogm	13 pt Fwgom	13 pt Fwgom
14 pt Fwogm	14 pt Fwgom	14 pt Fwgom
15 pt Fwogm	15 pt Fwgom	15 pt Fwgom
16 pt Fwogm	16 pt Fwgom	16 pt Fwgom
17 pt Fwogm	17 pt Fwgom	17 pt Fwgom
18 pt Fwogm	18 pt Fwgom	18 pt Fwgom
19 pt Fwogm	19 pt Fwgom	19 pt Fwgom
20 pt Fwogm	20 pt Fwgom	20 pt Fwgom
21 pt Fwogm	21 pt Fwgom	21 pt Fwgom
22 pt Fwogm	22 pt Fwgom	22 pt Fwgom
23 pt Fwogm	23 pt Fwgom	23 pt Fwgom
24 pt Fwogm	24 pt Fwgom	24 pt Fwgom

type styles

Every type family has various styles which differ in their stroke thickness, stroke lengths, and tracking. When a member of a type family is specified, the family name is given first, then the stroke thickness, then the type width and orientation, e.g. Times, bold, italic.

In computer typeface menus, there are various synonyms for type names. To make the names shorter or more uniform, the type styles are specified with numbers in some typefaces, e.g. Univers and Helvetica.

The Helvetica type family.

The "tens" describe the stroke thickness. For example 50 represents type styles with a normal line thickness, 20 stands for ultra-light, 30 for thin, 40 for light, 60 for medium (semi-bold), 70 for bold, 80 for heavy, and 90 for black (ultrabold).

The units describe the orientation and the width. The number 5 designates styles with a normal orientation and width. 3 designates extended styles, 7 stands for condensed styles, and 9 for extra condensed. The figure 6 stands for italic styles with a normal stroke thickness, 4 for italic styles with wide strokes, and 8 for italic styles with a narrow stroke.

Thus, Helvetica bold, extended, italic would be designated as Helvetica 74, Helvetica normal as Helvetica 55.

			extended	extended, italic	normal	normal, italic	condensed	condensed, italic	extra condensed
		_1	_2	_3	_4	_5	_6	_7	_8	_9
	1_								
ultra-light	2_			Mm	Mm	Mm	Mm	Mm	Mm	
thin	3_			Mm	Mm	Mm	Mm	Mm	Mm	
light	4_			Mm	Mm	Mm	Mm	Mm	Mm	
normal	5_			Mm	Mm	**Mm**	Mm	Mm	Mm	Mm
semi-bold	6_			Mm	Mm	Mm	Mm	Mm	Mm	
bold	7_			Mm	Mm	Mm	Mm	Mm	Mm	
heavy	8_			Mm	Mm	Mm	Mm	Mm	Mm	
ultrabold	9_			Mm	Mm	Mm	Mm	Mm	Mm	

Stroke thickness

ultralight
    extra light
    ultralight
thin
    thin
    light
normal
    book
    standard
    roman
semi-bold
    semi-bold
    medium
bold
    bold
    heavy
extra bold
    extra bold
    black
ultrabold
    black

Width

extra narrow
    extra condensed
    thin
narrow
    condensed
    compressed
    narrow
normal
    standard
wide
    expanded
    extended
extra wide
    extra expanded

Orientation

normal
    standard
italic
    italic
    oblique
    slanted

type styles
light, normal and bold

The suitability of different type styles such as light, normal and bold for use on the screen depends on the colors chosen for the type and the background. With a white or very light-colored screen background, the white or bright areas are much brighter than on paper because of the light generated by the color combination. This means that the edges of the type are obscured by "blooming", which makes the type appear thinner than it actually is. To counteract this blooming effect in text on the screen, it is possible to make the strokes slightly thicker.

A further possibility is to make the background darker or to select a dark shade of color as the background. Light typefaces, especially thin and ultralight styles, are therefore only suitable for the screen occasionally, and only in larger type sizes.

Normal styles, and especially bolder type styles, are well suited for use on the screen if the tracking is increased. The bolder the type style, the greater the tracking value should be.

If a typeface manufacturer provides bold type styles, these should be preferred to styles which are made bold by digital means. Like digitally italicized styles, digital bold styles can also appear unattractive and distorted.

Color and Type
Color and Type

Background white
Frutiger light blue 100 %, 20 pt, 11 pt

Color and Type
Color and Type

Background white
Frutiger normal blue 100 %, 20 pt, 11 pt

Color and Type
Color and Type

Background white
Frutiger semi-bold blue 100 %, 20 pt, 11 pt

Color and Type
Color and Type

Background white
Frutiger bold blue 100 %, 20 pt, 11 pt

Color and Type
Color and Type

Background white
Frutiger ultrabold blue 100 %, 20 pt, 11 pt

Color and Type
Color and Type

Background black, 100 %, Frutiger light
red 50 %, green 100 %, blue 50 %, 20 pt, 11 pt

Color and Type
Color and Type

Background black, 100 %, Frutiger normal
red 50 %, green 100 %, blue 50 %, 20 pt, 11 pt

Color and Type
Color and Type

Background black, 100 %, Frutiger semi-bold
red 50 %, green 100 %, blue 50 %, 20 pt, 11 pt

Color and Type
Color and Type

Background black, 100 %, Frutiger bold
red 50 %, green 100 %, blue 50 %, 20 pt, 11 pt

Color and Type
Color and Type

Background black, 100 %, Frutiger ultrabold
red 50 %, green 100 %, blue 50 %, 20 pt, 11 pt

type styles
italic, condensed, and extended

Color and Type in italic
Color and Type in italic

Background black 100%, Frutiger normal/italic
red 50%, green 100%, blue 50%, 20 pt, 11 pt

Color and Type in italic
Color and Type in italic

Background black 100%, Frutiger bold/italic
red 50%, green 100%, blue 50%, 20 pt, 11 pt

Color and type condensed
Color and type condensed

Background black 100%, Frutiger light/condensed
red 50%, green 100%, blue 50%, 20 pt, 11 pt

Color and type condensed
Color and type condensed

Background black 100%, Frutiger normal/condensed
red 50%, green 100%, blue 50%, 20 pt, 11 pt

Color and type condensed
Color and type condensed

Background black 100%, Frutiger bold/condensed
red 50%, green 100%, blue 50%, 20 pt, 11 pt

There are two ways of displaying an italic style (a typeface with oblique characters like handwriting): by using the italic style that has been specially developed by the typeface manufacturer, or by making the ordinary type oblique by digital means. A digitally oblique italic face has not been balanced out, and it can therefore sometimes look distorted. A characteristic of the italic style is that it has no vertical strokes; the "upright" strokes are usually at an angle of 12 or 12.5 degrees, or sometimes even 15 degrees. The pixel structure of the monitor thus creates "steps" which break letters down into a grid pattern and make them difficult to read. Even on paper, italic typefaces are used sparingly because they are tiring for the eyes. The grid pattern of the individual letters on the computer screen as a result of the oblique strokes is an additional factor.
So, italic type should be used even more sparingly on the screen than on paper and should be restricted to individual words.

Color and type with tracking
Color and type with tracking

Background black 100%, Univers normal, tracking + 10
red 50%, green 100%, blue 50%, 20 pt, 11 pt

Color and Type extended
Color and Type extended

Background black 100%, Univers normal/extended
red 50%, green 100%, blue 50%, 20 pt, 11 pt

Color and Type extended
Color and Type extended

Background black 100%, Univers bold/extended
red 50%, green 100%, blue 50%, 20 pt, 11 pt

Color and Type extended
Color and Type extended

Background black, 100%, Univers normal/extended/italic
red 50%, green 100%, blue 50%, 20 pt, 11 pt

The same applies to light typefaces. Even on paper these styles are only rarely used for longer texts. On the computer monitor, the poor resolution makes them difficult to read. At small sizes, light type styles can flow together. This not only impairs legibility, it also makes the overall design unattractive. One perfectly acceptable alternative on the computer screen is to use broad type styles. But these can appear clumsy, and a more attractive solution is to use a normal type style with an increased tracking value.

Color and Type
Color and Type

Color and Type
Color and Type

Type displayed on the screen is greatly
inferior in quality to printed type.
Printed type has a resolution of 1200
or 2400 dots per inch, compared with
the 72 dpi of the computer screen. Very
small type sizes (6 to 9pt), which are
perfectly legible on paper, are so
coarse in their resolution on the
screen that they can hardly be read.
Text on the screen should therefore be
at least 10 point, although text
between 11 and 14pt is better.
The corresponding title type size
should be between 14 and 20pt. In
choosing the size, the individual
typeface needs to be taken into
account.

Another factor to bear in mind is the
contrast between the type and the
background. If a light-colored type is
used on a darker screen background,
the type will appear slightly larger
and bolder than dark type on a
light-colored background.
In the first case, the light-colored type
"blooms" into the darker surrounding
color. In the second case, the type is
"bloomed" over by the light-colored
surrounding background.

This is a headline in 10 pt
Never use very small sizes for typography on the screen.
This text is in 7pt Geneva.

This is a headline in 12 pt
Never use very small sizes for typography on the screen.
This text is in 9 pt Geneva.
It is a comfortable size for reading on paper.

This is a headline in 14 pt
Never use very small sizes for typography on the screen.
This text is in 11 pt Geneva.
This should be the minimum size for text on screen.

This is a headline in 20 pt
Never use very small sizes for typography on the screen.
This text is in 14 pt Geneva.
It is a comfortable size for reading on the screen.

This is a headline in 20 pt
Never use very small sizes for typography on the screen.
This text is in 14 pt Geneva.
It is a comfortable size for reading on the screen.

m

cl

d

Text on the screen should always have a tracking of 5 to 10 units for improved legibility. Reducing the tracking will exacerbate the general problem that the letters on the screen appear too narrow. As a result, the letters may flow into each other and merge, so that unintended letters are sometimes seen. For example, if the letters "r" and "n" are set too close together, they may be read as an "m". When the letters "c" and "l" are set too close together, they appear like a "d". The same also applies to "o" and "l" when they are too close together. Bold type styles should have a generous tracking value in comparison with normal type styles.

But if the tracking is set too wide, the words will break up and the text will be difficult to read. The letter spacing for larger type sizes does not need to be increased in proportion with the increase in the type size. Larger type sizes need less tracking.

small sizes

Univers 14 pt, tracking of 10 units

small sizes

Univers 30 pt, tracking of 10 units

This text is set in 14 pt Univers Regular
with the character spacing set to -10.

This text is set in 14 pt Univers Regular
with standard character spacing.

This text is set in 14 pt Univers Regular
with the character spacing set to +5.

This text is set in 14 pt Univers Regular
with the character spacing set to +10.

This text is set in 14 pt Univers Regular
with the character spacing set to +25.

**This text is set in 14 pt Univers Black
with the character spacing set to -10.**

**This text is set in 14 pt Univers Black
with standard character spacing.**

**This text is set in 14 pt Univers Black
with the character spacing set to +5.**

**This text is set in 14 pt Univers Black
with the character spacing set to +10.**

**This text is set in 14 pt Univers Black
with the character spacing set to +25.**

interlinear spacing

Selecting the right interlinear spacing is vital for legibility and overall appearance. Texts that are set too tightly are unpleasant to read because the eye finds it difficult to find the beginning of the next line. If the interlinear spacing is too great, the reader will be distracted from the actual text by the large amount of white space.

The basic setting for interlinear spacing in the standard desktop publishing programs is about 120% of single line spacing and is called automatic line spacing, or "auto". The expression "single-line spacing" means that the descenders and ascenders of the characters on successive lines almost appear to touch.

On paper, automatic line spacing is a good basis to create pleasant legibility for texts with a moderate line length of about 55 characters per line. Texts in books are often set with line spacing of up to 140% because of the longer line lengths.

Interlinear spacing is an important element in making text easy to read, and it should be set to a more generous value on screen than for text on paper.

Given that about 35 characters per line is regarded as ideal on the screen, the line spacing should be set to about 150% or even greater. Here again, the general rule applies that if the lines are longer, the line spacing should also be greater.
Expanded or light type requires wider line spacing than narrow or bold type.

14pt x 120% = 16,8pt line spacing (auto)

14pt x 150% = 21pt line spacing

120%

Rules that apply to the use of typography and colour on paper do not necessarily apply on the computer screen, but they form a set of rules which can be used as a basis for alteration, and they provide the vocabulary that can be referred to. Different rules apply to improved legibility on the screen, and that applies particularly to the choice of typeface, the type size, the tracking and the use of line lengths and line spacing. Typefaces which were generally designed for print media show great weaknesses on modern 72 dpi monitors – they must not be used below a certain size and a certain tracking setting, which is greater than for print media, is essential if we wish to achieve maximum legibility.

150%

Rules that apply to the use of typography and colour on paper do not necessarily apply on the computer screen, but they form a set of rules which can be used as a basis for alteration, and they provide the vocabulary that can be referred to. Different rules apply to improved legibility on the screen, and that applies particularly to the choice of typeface, the type size, the tracking and the use of line lengths and line spacing. Typefaces which were generally designed for print media show great weaknesses on modern 72 dpi monitors – they must not be used below a certain size and a certain tracking setting, which is greater than for print media, is essential if we wish to achieve maximum legibility.

line length

In addition to the selection of a suitable typeface, there are other ways to make reading on the screen easier. On paper, for example, 35 – 55 characters per line are regarded as ideal depending on type size and line width. On the screen, the maximum is 35 characters, or even less. But the lines must not be so short that there is sometimes only a single word in a line, or that too many words are hyphenated. Unless it is deliberately done for effect, it is important to avoid the impression of a vertical arrangement of characters (like Chinese script) in lines that are too short with line spacing that is too large.

The line length must always be seen in relation to the line spacing. The greater the line spacing, the longer the lines can be – and vice versa.

Geneva, 14pt

10   20

In addition to the selection of a suitable typeface, there are also other methods to facilitate reading on the screen. On paper, for example, 35 - 55 characters per line are regarded as ideal. On the screen, the maximum is 35 characters, or even less.

Geneva, 14pt

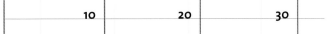

In addition to the selection of
a suitable typeface, there are
also other methods to facilitate
reading on the screen. On paper,
for example, 35 – 55 characters
per line are regarded as ideal.
On the screen, the maximum is
35 characters, or even less.

Geneva, 14pt

In addition to the selection of a suitable typeface, there
are also other methods to facilitate reading on the
screen. On paper, for example, 35 – 55 characters per
line are regarded as ideal. On the screen, the maximum
is 35 characters, or even less.

text quantity on the screen

When beginning to design a page on the screen, a background grid makes it easier to organize the text and pictures. With a grid, the design becomes coherent. The text quantity, the number of columns and their relationship to each other, the column width, and the position of the pictures are defined, to name just a few of the most important elements.
The reader will find it easier to follow the structure of successive pages if the text is organised in this way.

When a grid like this is created, it is important to remember that the reader should not be expected to deal with too much text on the screen. The poor resolution of the screen by comparison with paper means that the type size and interlinear spacing need to be larger.
Depending on the type size and the interlinear spacing, the text should not have more than 10 to 25 lines for each section. The less text, the better. If the type is large, the text blocks can have more lines. These short text blocks can be distributed around the page without seeming to be isolated from each other. In this case, a grid is particularly useful.
In exceptional cases, a whole page can be filled with text, but then the possibility arises that the reader will quickly become tired or bored.

To preserve the reader's momentum, it is helpful if large blocks of text can be broken up. This can be done by sub-headings, or on a screen it can be done by color-coded "hotwords". These stand out and act as landmarks helping the reader to find his or her way around the text. In contrast with printing on paper, the cost of an additional color is not a factor here. Many multimedia programs offer functions to create "hotwords". These hotwords describe a subject in the document or an important word which, when clicked on, will provide additional information or change the level. The choice of color should be made very carefully to ensure that the overall design is attractive and that no flickering arises from the color contrasts.

The smaller the type size, the shorter the text blocks should be.

First example
This is a short text in the typeface
Univers 55.
The type size is 14 point with a
line length of about 35 characters
per line.

Second example
This is a short text in the typeface
Univers 55.
The type size is 18 point with a
line length of about 35 characters
per line.

The use of script typefaces on the screen raises the same issues as italic type and serif typefaces.

Script typefaces are characterized by such features as varying stroke widths and oblique letters which are very similar to handwritten texts.

The narrow strokes and the oblique orientation of the individual letters are unsuitable for display on the screen.

The pixel-based display breaks thin strokes, often making them indistinguishable, and in extreme cases they even disappear completely.

Even on paper, the many available script typefaces are only rarely used. On the computer screen they should be avoided completely.

Highlighting forms such as outline or shadow type are usually avoided on paper in spite of the high resolution. On the screen they are not advisable for functional reasons.

96

Outline — Frutiger Bold

Outline — Geneva

Outline

Outline

Shadow — Frutiger Bold

Shadow — Geneva

Shadow

Shadow

highlighting typefaces

Arcadia

Blur

The difficulty with outline type styles lies in the thin lines. The typeface looks dirty because the thin lines are shown with a heavy pixel structure. When shadowed styles are used, the shadow is hardly seen. On the screen, the effect of shading tends to be to make the characters appear fuzzy. This applies especially to smaller type sizes.

Experimental typefaces are often hardly legible even on paper. They are often rather expressionistic and abstract, and are used mainly when legibility is less of a priority than speed of recognition and the creation of a visual identity.

The computer is a good medium to follow the rapidly changing trends in experimental typefaces at moderate cost. They need to be used very sparingly, however – for example, as an eye-catcher for individual words or symbols. Whether a particular typeface is suitable for a particular context must be a matter of individual judgement.

Zapf Ch

Zapf Chancery

Zapf Chancery

Kuenstler Script

Kuenstler Script

FLIGHTCASE

harting

industria

Troubador

Wilhelm Klingspor Got

Antique or serif typefaces should be used sparingly on the screen because, after a time, with longer texts, they become hard to read. Although serif typefaces are used everyday in newspapers all over the world, they cannot simply be transferred to the computer, for example, for use in an "electronic newspaper".

The main reason for this is the varying thickness of the strokes that make up the letter, and the rounded nature of the serifs themselves.

Capital letters such as E, F, H, I, L and T are characterized by the purely rectilinear strokes.
That means that these letters in grotesque type will fit perfectly in the square grid which makes up the screen, and do not have ragged edges. In the same letters in an antique typeface, the serifs incorporate curves, leading to a ragged edge structure. Antique type therefore does not appear as smooth as a grotesque typeface. And the smaller the letter and the type size become, the more the characters will look like a bitmap typeface.

EFHILT

EFHILT

T T

AKMNVWXY

AKMNVWXY

Capital letters such as A, K, M, N, V, W,
X, and Y are characterized by their
oblique strokes.
In antique typefaces, these oblique
strokes vary in width. Where the
strokes are very thin, they could be
visually dominated by the thicker
strokes. This impression is heightened
in very thin strokes because of the
pixel structure on both sides, which
means that there is hardly any "meat"
in between.

Letters with round forms such as B, C,
D, G, O, P, Q, R, and S normally show up
badly on the screen.

Antique typefaces should therefore
not be chosen for long texts on the
screen, and never in small type sizes.
When choosing between several
antique typefaces, it is important to
ensure that the serifs and strokes are
not too thin.

t l f i h

t l f i h

BCDGOPQRS

BCDGOPQRS

OO

RR

DISK ECONOMY

5

AND TYPEFACES

On the 72 dpi monitors in general use today, round and oblique type forms are displayed with a distinctly jagged edge.

These "steps" can be balanced by smoothing the type. In the round and oblique parts of the letters, i.e. where the "steps" occur, intermediate color values are calculated when a typeface is smoothed.

If smoothed text is greatly magnified, the individual letters look fuzzy and distorted. At the original size, however, the human eye is unable to detect this distortion, and automatically "rounds off" the edges, so that the text appears to have smooth contours. Bitmap fonts such as Geneva and Chicago should not be smoothed. Bitmap typefaces do not need to be calculated by the computer because they are already available in pixel form. The disadvantage is that these typefaces can only be displayed in type sizes for which there is a bitmap if they are to generate a clear type impression.

Outline typefaces are contained in separately stored files as contours or outlines with real curves. The computer then fills in these curves with pixels in order to create a satisfactory image on the screen. If the type size is increased, the outlines are increased in proportion and filled in with a correspondingly greater number of pixels.

Outline typefaces are particularly commonly used in databases because of the small amount of memory which they require.

BeBox

Epsi Sans

E-World Tight

Tecton

Chicago

Geneva

102

On the 72 dpi monitors which
are in use today, round and
oblique type forms are displayed with a distinctly jagged
edge. These »steps« can be
balanced by smoothing the
type. In the round and oblique
parts of the letters, i.e. where
the »steps« occur, intermediate colour values are calculated
when a typeface is smoothed.
If smoothed text is greatly
magnified, the individual letters look fuzzy and distorted.
At the original size, however,
our eyes are unable to detect
this distortion because they
automatically close the round
shapes by means of the intermediate levels. The result
is a text which apparently has
smooth contours.

Bitmap fonts such as Geneva
and Chicago should not be
smoothed.

On the 72 dpi monitors which
are in use today, round and
oblique type forms are displayed with a distinctly jagged
edge. These »steps« can be
balanced by smoothing the
type. In the round and oblique
parts of the letters, i.e. where
the »steps« occur, intermediate colour values are calculated
when a typeface is smoothed.
If smoothed text is greatly
magnified, the individual letters look fuzzy and distorted.
At the original size, however,
our eyes are unable to detect
this distortion because they
automatically close the round
shapes by means of the intermediate levels. The result
is a text which apparently has
smooth contours.

Bitmap fonts such as Geneva
and Chicago should not be
smoothed.

Univers 14 pt, unsmoothed

Univers 14 pt, smoothed

104

The memory required by typefaces can be a problem with large files or interactive systems with computers with a small amount of RAM memory. Elements such as pictures or typefaces which need a lot of memory may make it much slower to load files.

Typefaces which have been smoothed with an image processing program are then stored as pictures, rather than as typefaces. The advantage of a smoothed typeface is that it creates a particularly good screen display with soft curves, but the disadvantage is that this form of type presentation requires a great deal of memory. A further disadvantage (although this too can sometimes be an advantage) is that smoothed typefaces cannot be edited or changed in any way. This means that it is not possible to copy, mark, increase the size, or change the style of the smoothed text displayed.

As the text in its smoothed form is now stored as a picture, someone reading these texts does not need to load the typeface into his or her system. If typefaces are sent separately in a suitcase, permission to use them must be obtained from the typeface manufacturers.

Serif typefaces, however, should not be smoothed in small type sizes because this could make the downstrokes disappear.

unsmoothed typefaces

Bitmap typefaces do not need much memory because only one bit per pixel is required to display them.
This bit decides whether a pixel lights up or not. If such "genuine" typefaces are used, i.e. typefaces which are not stored as pictures, the text can be edited. Because of the pixel structure of such typefaces on the screen they should not be used at small type sizes. It is advisable to use a type size of at least 14pt.

If further parameters such as color, tracking, etc., are assigned to such a typeface, this correspondingly increases the amount of memory the computer needs to perform each operation.

"Genuine" typefaces are also used if the user of a document can make entries in a window. It is impossible to make entries in a smoothed form.

The number of typefaces installed on a computer system also affects how quickly a file can be opened. The more typefaces are installed on the system, the longer the computer will take to start the relevant program. In this case, the computer must first refer back to an extensive type menu.

6

EXAMPLES

project
bundespreis (federal prize)
type
Univers 55, 14pt, 18pt, 28pt
Univers 65
comment
To present a medical instrument, it was important to have a clinically white background. A relatively generous type size with large interlinear spacing prevents the text from becoming illegible as a result of blooming.

Der Rat für Formgebung präsentiert :
The German Design Council presents :

bundespreis produktdesign **1996**

Deutsch   English

Precision Ergonomics

The **resectoscope** is an endoscopic medical **instrument** for carrying out **operations** on the prostate gland.

OES 4000 Resectoscope
Olympus Winter & Ibe GmbH
Design: Fred Held, Windi Winderlich Design

bundespreis produktdesign **1996**

An overview of
the award-winning products

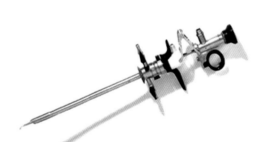

OES 4000 **Resektoskop**
Olympus Winter & Ibe GmbH

bundespreis produktdesign **1996**

An overview of
the award-winning products

DESIGN REAL INFORMATION DESIGN

□ □ □ □

U.R.L.

 P R O J E C T S

Komplettlösungen

In|di|vi|dua|li|tät *die*; -, -en: [franz.] (Einzigartigkeit
der Persönlichkeit [nur *Sing.*]);
→ in|di|vi|duel|le Lö|sung: (Spezialität von U.R.L.)

FontShop Österreich
Alle Schriften dieser Welt.

FontShop Deutschland
Wir bringen Schrift zur Sprache.

MEGO / M.DOS
Its all perfectly simple.

EUnet Österreich
Österreichs internationaler Service-Provider.

FUSE 95
The Forum For Experimental Typography.

Codico
The Component Distributing Company.

ABOUT | PROJECTS | SERVICES | CONTACT

concept
design
technology

U.R.L.

Das Web Competence Center

project
URL – Web Competence Center
type
Interstate Light, 11pt, 15pt, 17pt
Serifa Black 65pt, 72pt
comment
The generous type sizes of the headlines and sub-
headings here are attractive. The actual message is
set in blue, which is easy to read against the white
background. The subject areas are set in gray. The
danger of insufficient contrast with the light-
coloured background is avoided by the use of a
bold style and a larger type size.

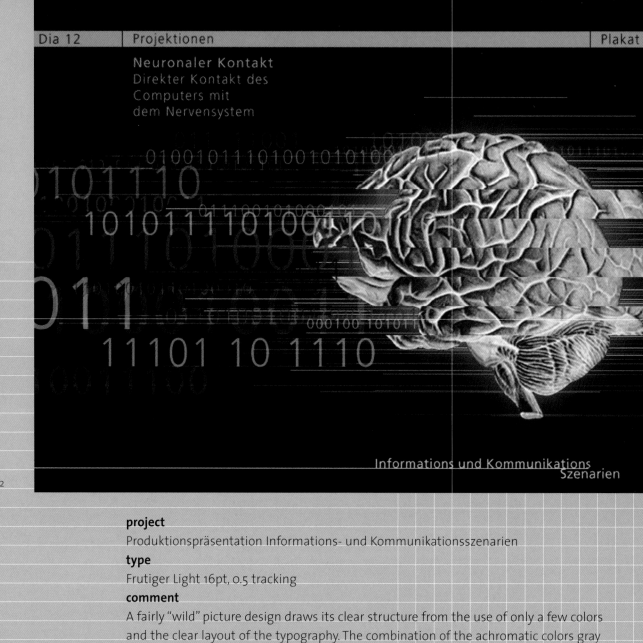

Neuronaler Kontakt
Direkter Kontakt des
Computers mit
dem Nervensystem

Informations und Kommunikations
Szenarien

112

project
Produktionspräsentation Informations- und Kommunikationsszenarien
type
Frutiger Light 16pt, 0.5 tracking
comment
A fairly "wild" picture design draws its clear structure from the use of only a few colors and the clear layout of the typography. The combination of the achromatic colors gray and black with orange creates a pleasant overall impression.

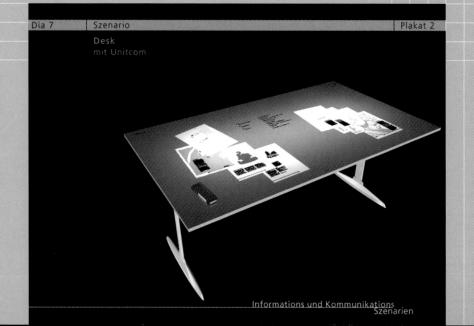

Desk
mit Unitcom

Informations und Kommunikations
Szenarien

Emotionaler Kontakt
Annähernde
Vermenschlichung
des Computers

Informations und Kommunikations
Szenarien

DESIGN ANTHONY CHRISTENSEN DAVID KREBS

Dia 10 | Projektionen | Plakat 1

Interaktion
Durch Aktion und
Reaktion bestimmte
Verbindung

12345 16789 8

Informations und Kommunikations
Szenarien

Das Barbie Syndrom
Brauchen MSdchen wirklich ihr eigenes Zelt dort drauβen im dunklen und gefShrlichen Wald der Computerspiele?
> >> read.only.media

.r.o.m.
.archiv
.reviews
.com
.we.care

.buzz

re.buzz -> elektronische lebensaspekte

binary.continuous.mode.97

-> **rom**. "read only media" in ganzen Worten. Unsere, sowie Eure Schnittstelle zum Glück. Ein ganz wunderbar heiterer Mix feat. Texte, Artikel, Kolumnen, Besprechungen, Crap, Morons, Ultra.
Das Spektrum der Aspekte, die wir meinen. Denn der Text ist unsere Party (oder Eure?).

..............................-> go there!.

project
Buzz
type
Base 9sc, 20pt

comment
For the background, colors have been selected with muted tone values which are close together, producing an attractive overall effect. Individual elements in orange appear all the more refreshing.

.r.o.m.
archiv
reviews
.com
.we.care

.buzz

re.buzz -> elektronische lebensaspekte   binary.continuous.mode.97

-> rom. "read only media" in ganzen Worten. Unsere, sowie Eure Schnittstelle zum Glück. Ein ganz wunderbar heiterer Mix feat. Texte, Artikel, Kolumnen, Besprechungen, Crap, Morons, Ultra.
Das Spektrum der Aspekte, die wir meinen. Denn der Text ist unsere Party (oder Eure?).

...............................**-> go there!**

-> archiv. alle Texte bis jetzt und die da kommen werden.

...............................**-> go there!**

-> reviews. Null und Eins Musik im Glanze ganzer Journalistengenrationen. 150 until now, darfs noch etwas mehr sein?.

...............................**-> go there!**

-> com. Der re.buzz Strip. (pornographic communication included). Dialogische Optionen zur Probe, Kampf der Lethagie!

...............................**-> go there!**

-> we care. .. und wie. copy paste in Anwendung lernen und umsetzen. Dem Grundgutem zuliebe

...............................**-> go there!**

115

DESIGN ALEXANDER BAUMGARDT, JAN RIKUS HILLMANN,
VICKY TIEGELKAMP

project
The component distributing company
type
Can you read me, 22pt
Plate 32pt
Engraves Gothic 14pt
comment
Deep blue and a modern typeface are used to portray a technological image. The body text is also set in blue rather than black. This does not create any interfering contrast with the white background. But the color is only really noticeable in the bold words. Red is reserved for the key words which refer to the following pages.

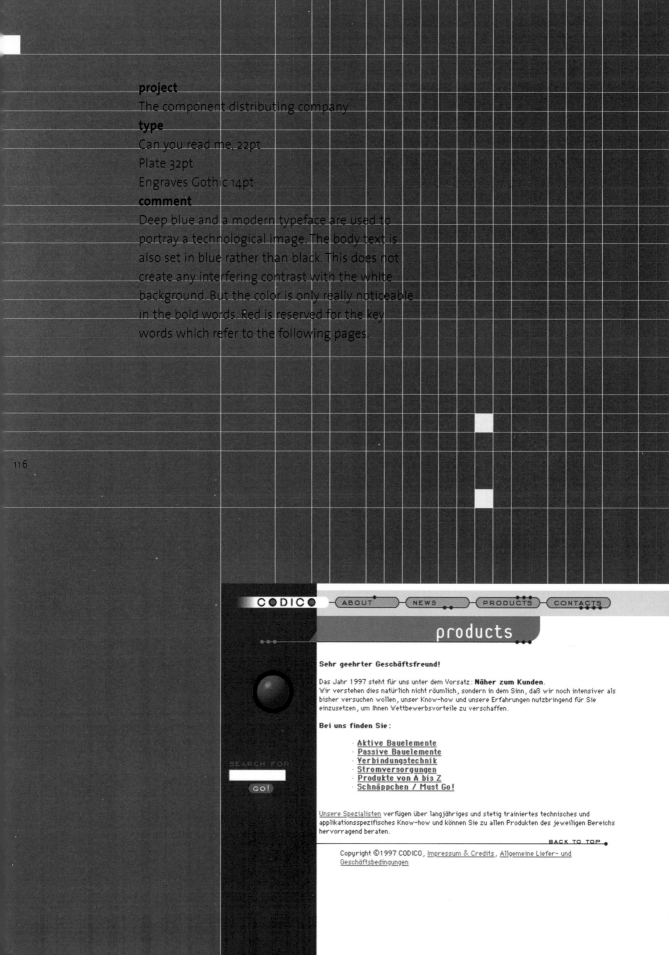

CODICO ABOUT NEWS PRODUCTS CONTACTS

products

Sehr geehrter Geschäftsfreund!

Das Jahr 1997 steht für uns unter dem Vorsatz: **Näher zum Kunden**.
Wir verstehen dies natürlich nicht räumlich, sondern in dem Sinn, daß wir noch intensiver als bisher versuchen wollen, unser Know-how und unsere Erfahrungen nutzbringend für Sie einzusetzen, um Ihnen Wettbewerbsvorteile zu verschaffen.

Bei uns finden Sie:

- **Aktive Bauelemente**
- **Passive Bauelemente**
- **Verbindungstechnik**
- **Stromversorgungen**
- **Produkte von A bis Z**
- **Schnäppchen / Must Go!**

Unsere Spezialisten verfügen über langjähriges und stetig trainiertes technisches und applikationsspezifisches Know-how und können Sie zu allen Produkten des jeweiligen Bereichs hervorragend beraten.

BACK TO TOP

Copyright ©1997 CODICO, Impressum & Credits, Allgemeine Liefer- und Geschäftsbedingungen

SEARCH FOR:

GO!

WELCOME TO

CODICO®

THE COMPONENT DISTRIBUTING COMPANY
Smart products for the industry – check us out!

ABOUT

NEWS

PRODUCTS

CONTACTS

Go

SEARCH FOR

weiter in Deutsch ▶

DESIGN U.R.L.

DESIGN VIRTUAL IDENTITY

ensburger®

▶ ▶ ▶ neu
▼

neue pressetexte®:
music collection
zaubern

Pink Panther :
neue topagenten

ving Puzzle
oving Puzzle

THINK.

Käpt'n Blaubär
   die wahre Geschichte
   des Internets...
Special
   Pink Panther zu
   Besuch bei Ravensburger
Intergame
   Spiel zur Site...

Produkte
   die schönsten Bücher,
   Spiele und CD-Roms...

Service
   Wir sind ansprechbar...
Gutenacht
   täglich eine neue
   Gutenachtgeschichte
Presse
   News von Ravensburger

7 Ravensburger AG ®

project
Ravensburger Spiele
type
Futura, Meta, Helvetica, Courier, 12pt
comment
To make it attractive to children as well as adults and generally to convey the image of a toy manufacturer, a large number of colors have been used and the key words are highlighted with colors rather than just underlining.

Flickering of the transition between the type and the background is avoided by not using contrasts that are too harsh. A blue background is more suitable for white type than a black background.

gute nacht
geschichte

Nortrud Boge-Erli:

Trostlied von den Sternen
....

Bist hingefalln? Hat's weh getan?
Und mußt du jetzt gleich weinen?
Komm her zu mir, denk nicht mehr dran
erzähl dir was vom kleinen
vom kleinen Bär
vom großen Bär
von mitten in der Nacht:
im Sternkleid tanzt der große Bär
im Sternkleid tanzt der kleine Bär
den Himmel lang
und lacht.

Aus: **Mein Buch der Gutenachtgeschichten**,
Hrsg. von Sabine Schuler, Ravensburger Buchverlag 1996

© 1997 Ravensburger AG

video
online

video.1
986k
(in studio)
03.March.97

Video
18.06.97

purity:

Jill Stark - programming / production / vocals / guitars
Icy Lazare - keyboards / Samplers / bass guitar
Florence Briggs - samplers/ live mix + guitars

purity combine a mixture of full-on programming using drum'n' bass and breakbeat influences, with played in keyboards & samplers .... fused with wall-of-noise guitars, bass and weird vocals.

From a background of programming, studio recording, and playing guitar/sequencers in previous bands - Jill Stark now writes, programmes, produces and engineers all the purity material.

Jill Stark : interview (coming soon)

DESIGN ANONYMOUS BAND SUPPORTER FROM ENGLAND

project
purity music
comment
Gray type on a black background has a similar effect to white type but avoids the disadvantages of blooming. This enables the type to be set at a smaller size than would normally be required for screen display.

FontShop

FontShop

BookShop

SchriftMuster 3

zurück weiter

FUSE

Seit 5 Jahren erschüttert FUSE die Typo-Szene: Experimentelle Schriften, ausgewählt von Neville Brody und Jon Wozencroft. Hier vier Klassiker:

F Moonbase Alpha: Cornell Windlin

ABCDEFGHIJKLMNOP
QRSTUVWXYZabcdef
ghijklmnopqrstuvwx
çânöü!$¥??123456789

F Scratched Out: Pierre di Scullio

Nicht alles aber die wichtigen und aktuellen Klassiker.

Hier acht Bestseller aus unserem Angebot:

1 Thomas Merz
Die PostScript- & Acrobat-Bibel

Was sie schon immer über PostScript und Acrobat/PDF wissen wollten.

2 Erik Spiekermann

122

FontShop

Alle Schriften dieser Welt: vollständig, übersichtlich, von Experten ausgewählt, sofort lieferbar. Nur Originalschriften, keine Helveticos oder Frutussis. Das FontBook zeigt die Bibliotheken von 50 großen und kleinen Herstellern, alphabetisch und nach Stil sortiert.

Zudem führt FontShop mit der FontFont-Bibliothek und FUSE eigene, exklusive Schriften. Für Kunden in Osteuropa bietet FontShop Fremdsprachenschriften und kyrillische Fonts. Logos, Symbole und Dingbats-Sammlungen runden das Schriftenprogramm ab.

1 URW Traffic Collection

Alle Verkehrszeichen der Straßenverkehrsordnung (StVO), handdigitalisiert nach Originalvorlagen: Gebote, Verbote, Warnungen, Hinweise, Pfeile und Symbole sowie Beispiele für Textschilder. Vierfarbige Illustrator-Dateien, für PC und Mac. Zehn Verkehrsschriften im PostScript und TrueType-Format.

2 FontFont

Vor rund 6 Jahren gründete FSI, FontShop International, die exklusive FontFont-Bibliothek. Heute gibt es 900 FontFonts, neben Verrücktheiten viele anspruchsvolle Textschriften, Symbol-Fonts, kyrillische Versionen und technische Kuriositäten, wie zum Beispiel die Random-Schriften.

3 FUSE

heißt die bei FontShop vierteljährlich erscheinende Sammlung experimenteller Schriften. Die FUSE-Redakteure Neville Brody, John Critchley und Jon Wozencroft laden internationale Designer ein, eine Schrift und ein Poster zu einem festgelegten Thema zu entwerfen.

4 FontHits

Professionelle Schriften müssen nicht teuer sein. Viele Hersteller bieten preiswerte Font- Zusammenstellungen an. FontShop hat sie alle gesammelt und in der FontHits-Broschüre zusammengefaßt. Kostenlos, gleich bestellen: Klick.

project
Fontshop
type
FF Meta, 24pt, 48pt

---

zur Weiterbildung für Schriftenfreunde – und die

Richard Saul Wurmann
Information Architects

Nur wer komplexe Sachverhalte klar vermitteln kann, wird im Informationszeitalter vorankommen. Richard Saul Wurmann, Architekt und seit Jahren auch Fachautor und Konferenzveranstalter, stellt weltweit führende Informations-Designer und deren Arbeiten vor. Darunter Bruce Robertson (Diagramm, London), Richard Curtis (USA today, Arlington) und Erik Spiekermann (MetaDesign, Berlin). Lernen Sie das Louvre-Orientierungssystem genauer kennen oder die preisgekrönten Schautafeln des American Museum of Natural History.

236 Seiten, gebunden, 600 vierfarbige Abbildungen. Graphis Press, Zürich 1996.

David Carson.

F YoucanReadMe: Phil Baines

FUSE erscheint vierteljährlich in limitierter Auflage und kostet DM 130,– (DM 110,– im Abo). Die hier gezeigten FUSE-Schriften wurden als überarbeitete FontFonts im Paket FUSE Classics 1 wiederveröffentlicht.

Fuse Classics 1 :
FF 9926 Mac oder PC, DM 289,– inkl. MwSt.

---

comment
The yellow background gives a dynamic impression, and in combination with the black type it stands out. Other chromatic colors are only used very deliberately in specific places, for example in the menu bar. If the red were used for longer text lines it would blur with the yellow because of their proximity in the color circle.

project
Aeonflux
type
OCR A 65pt (icons), Geneva

comment
White type is easy to read if the background colour with a medium intrinsic brightness (e.g., green or red) is darkened slightly. The resulting contrast is strong enough for the letters to be clearly recognized, but not strong enough for blooming to occur.

eat my binary, bastard !!!

SCHUBKRAFT BUSINESS

central message:

TVSUCKER

secundo:
No sense = nonsense
no links, no bookmarks
(just crap, morons, ultra)
basskraft 9000. ultimative energie.

DESIGN AEONFLUX

best results with Netscape 1.1
zur visuellen erbauung

[ATOMIC RETRO BASS SYSTEM]

secundo:
music research in breakbeat and jungle
all hardcore styles in unique ways
(a kind of secret aural technology and mechanical organics)

project
drum and bass
comment
If key words are to be used on a web
page, it does not necessarily mean
that they must be set in a completely
different color to be noticed.

The left text block, with about 30
characters per line, is far easier to read
than the top text block, with about 70
characters per line.

DRUM 'N' BASS

DRUM 'N' BASS

DRUM 'N' BASS

'N' BASS.

THE COOLEST BREAK BEAT SITE ON THE NET

Teebone is one of the youngest and most respected DJ producers on the Drum
and Bass scene. Collaborated artists is the first of his productions, in what
will be a series of albums. This first album is a testament to his rising
profile, which has been achieved through individual creativity and building on
a sound network of like-minded artists, dedicated to producing high quality
music.

is is just the first incarnation
the catalogue section.
've got six labels up at present
d more will be arriving soon.

THE COOLEST BREAKBEAT SITE ON THE NET

JUNGLE MASSIVE JUNGLE MASSIVE JUNGLE MASSIVE JUNGLE MASSIVE

FEATURED ARTIST

Teebone is one of the youngest and most respected DJ producers on the Drum and Bass scene. Collaborated artists is the first of his productions, in what will be a series of albums. This first album is a testament to his rising profile, which has been achieved through individual creativity and building on a sound network of like-minded artists, dedicated to producing high quality music.

ORDER DIRECT

CATALOGUE

This is just the first incarnation of the catalogue section.
We've got six labels up at present and more will be arriving soon.

Shiny Beast

certificate eighteen

RIDDIM TRACK

DJS, INTERVIEWS, REVIEWS

FEATURES

Check out the latest reviews, international DJ's run us through their sets. Or soak up some serious info from interviews with the cream of the Drum 'n' Bass world, from Booming Bukem to Spring Heel Jack or the jazz mayhem of Photek.

CLUBS, LISTINGS, LINKS

SCENE

Get an update on the best clubs around as well as live event listings. Browse or download our cool flyer collection. Link to other fine sites.

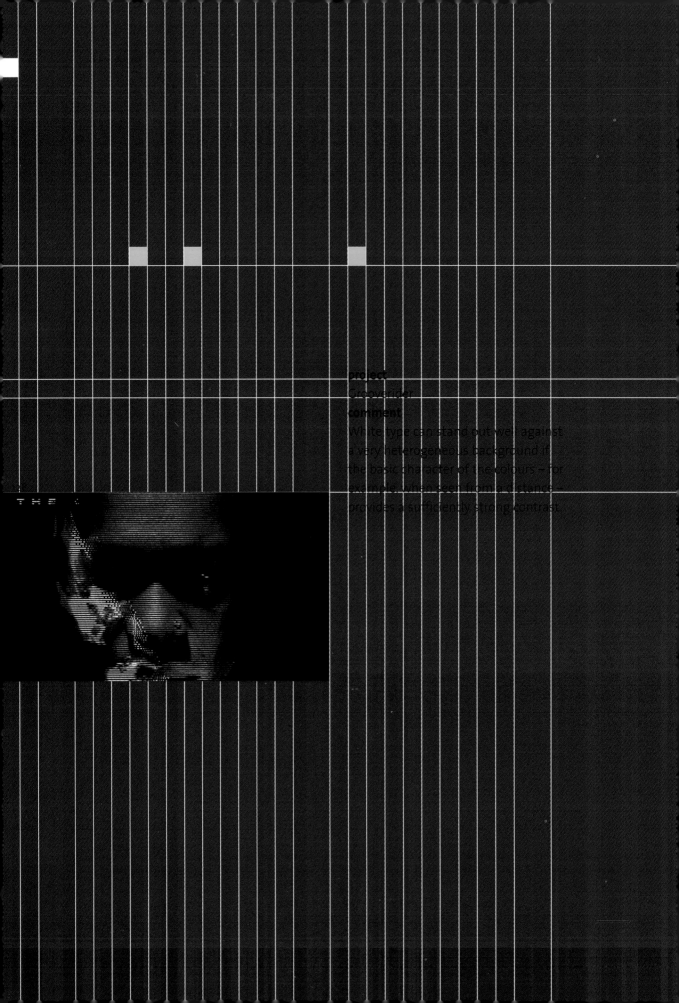

project
Grooverider

comment
White type can stand out well against
a very heterogeneous background if
the basic character of the colours – for
example when seen from a distance –
provides a sufficiently strong contrast.

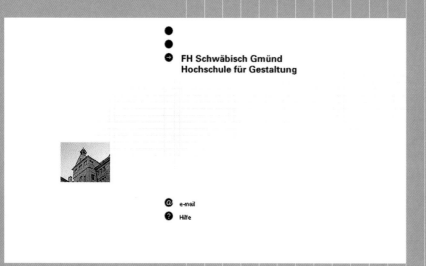

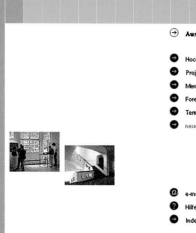

project
HfG
type
1. page Univers, smoothed
Folgeseiten Helvetica 12pt

comment

Black type on a white background is reasonable for text on the screen as long as it is only used – as here – for single words and pages without too much text. The most important and "urgent" key word is marked in red. On the following pages, with a larger amount of text, white on black is used.

DESIGN DETLEF BURSIEK, ALEXANDER KRENZ, HEIKO MATTERN
MATHIAS RISCHEWSKI, STUDIENGANG VISUELLE GESTALTUNG 7

METALHEADZ

SOUNDS

SCENES

THE ARTISTS

INFO

CLUB SESSIONS

MERCHANDISE

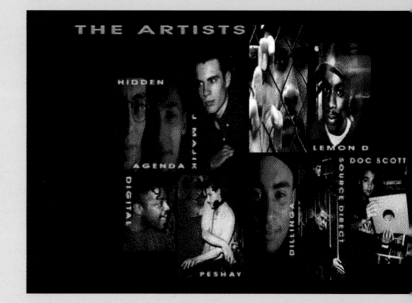

THE ARTISTS

HIDDEN

J MAJIK

LEMON D

AGENDA

DIGITAL

DOC SCOTT

SOURCE DIRECT

DILLINGA

PESHAY

132

DILLINGA

This 26 year old from Clapham is probably among the youngest DJ's to evolve out of Jungle and of course on to the Metalheadz label.

Real name Carl practises good sounds and bass at home on his computer, with the help of an amp and a keyboard Dillinja can create a unique style of jungle that is individual to the industry. [More]

TRACK SAMPLES

PRESS CUTTINGS

CLUB SESSIONS SCENES SOUNDS MERCHANDISE ARTISTS HOME

INFO

project
Metalhead
comment
Secondary colors such as turquoise can appear quite striking if they
are used against a muted, dark background. A slight flicker causes the
turquoise type to come to the foreground, whereas the white type of
the key words appears to be on the same level as the background.

134

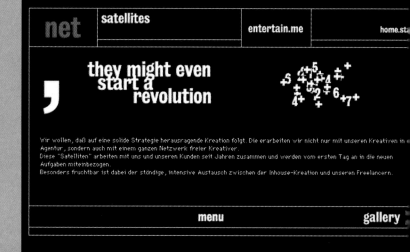

they might even
start a
revolution

Wir wollen, daß auf eine solide Strategie herausragende Kreation folgt. Die erarbeiten wir nicht nur mit unseren Kreativen in
Agentur, sondern auch mit einem ganzen Netzwerk freier Kreativer.
Diese "Satelliten" arbeiten mit uns und unseren Kunden seit Jahren zusammen und werden vom ersten Tag an in die neuen
Aufgaben miteinbezogen.
Besonders fruchtbar ist dabei der ständige, intensive Austausch zwischen der Inhouse-Kreation und unseren Freelancern.

net   satellites   entertain.me   home.sta

menu   gallery

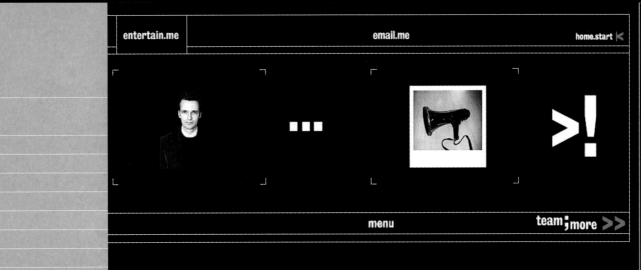

menu

team;more >>

project
start
type
Bureau Grotesk 37, Frutiger Roman

135

comment
Small white type against a black background appears darker
than larger, bold white type because too much light emanating
from the screen will create blooming. Black/red/white is
well-known as a seductive color combination.

the unauthorised , photoalbum

,

"

Pictures to end careers. You are one of the few see them. For safety
reasons, these pages should be equipped with a hypnosis protector. In 10
minutes you will not remember anything.

menu

[... ,   >>

menu

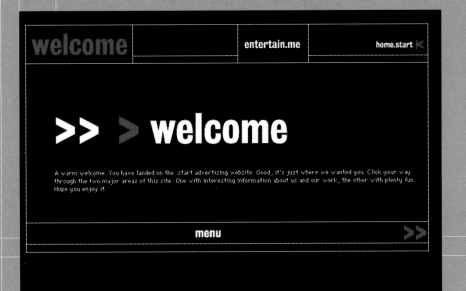

welcome

entertain.me

home.start

>> > **welcome**

A warm welcome. You have landed on the .start advertising website. Good, it's just where we wanted you. Click your way through the two major areas of this site: One with interesting information about us and our work, the other with plenty fun. Hope you enjoy it.

menu >>

DESIGN START

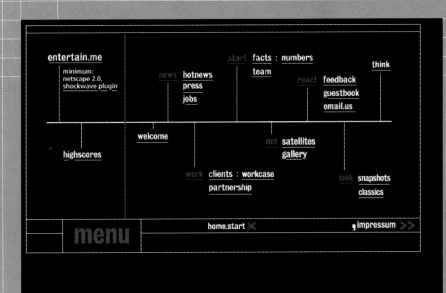

entertain.me

minimum: netscape 2.0, shockwave plugin

news **hotnews** **press** **jobs**

.start **facts : numbers** **team**

react **feedback** **guestbook** **email.us**

think

highscores

welcome

net **satellites** **gallery**

work **clients : workcase** **partnership**

look **snapshots** **classics**

menu home.start impressum >>

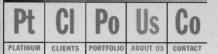
PLATINUM DESIGN IS AN AWARD-WINNING GRAPHIC DESIGN FIRM THAT PROVIDES ITS CLIENTS WITH INTELLIGENT, INNOVATIVE COMMUNICATION STRATEGIES. FOR TWELVE YEARS WE HAVE SPECIALIZED IN PROBLEM-SOLVING, LOOKING AT THE TOTAL PICTURE AND OFFERING YOU A SOLUTION THAT CONSIDERS THE GENESIS OF THE PROBLEM, ITS OVERALL OBJECTIVES, AND THE EXPECTATIONS OF YOUR AUDIENCE.

PLATINUM ACHIEVES THESE OBJECTIVES BY OFFERING A WIDE RANGE OF SERVICES, INCLUDING: CORPORATE COMMUNICATIONS, PROMOTIONAL CAMPAIGNS, MEDIA AND SALES KITS, BOOK AND EDITORIAL DESIGN, AND PACKAGING DESIGN.

DESIGN PLATINUM

138

FLEXIBILITY SUPPORTS EMERGING BUSINESS NEEDS

When K-III Communications wanted a striking graphic identity for their new magazine division, entitled K-III Magazines, Platinum's in-depth knowledge of the publishing industry made it the design firm of choice.

PLATINUM

BRILLIANT
COMMUNICATION
STRATEGIES

Pt	Cl	Po	Us	Co
PLATINUM	CLIENTS	PORTFOLIO	ABOUT US	CONTACT

project
platinum
type
Syntax, 12pt
comment
Large line spacing and about 40 characters per line ensure good legibility. Orange key words on a white background appear more restrained because the white blooms over the orange and because the two colors have similar levels of intrinsic brightness. The look of the page is also enhanced by the small number of elements used.

White type on an orange background appears comparatively strong. Blooming gives it a greater weight than it would have on paper.

Corporate

> click on image for a closer look

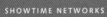

SCHLESINGER ASSOCIATES

SHOWTIME NETWORKS

PFIZER INC

K-III MAGAZINE GROUP

HOME | CLIENTS | PORTFOLIO | ABOUT US | CONTACT

welcome
| english | deutsch | français |
vitra.

products
designers & architects
architecture
news
addresses
feedback
vitra design museum
vitra the company

project
vitra
type
Futura Bold, 12pt, 0.5 tracking

comment
Gray text on a black background is effective but it must be sufficiently bold, as here, in order to be effective. To avoid too harsh a contrast of black and white, the white has been concentrated with a smaller percentage of yellow

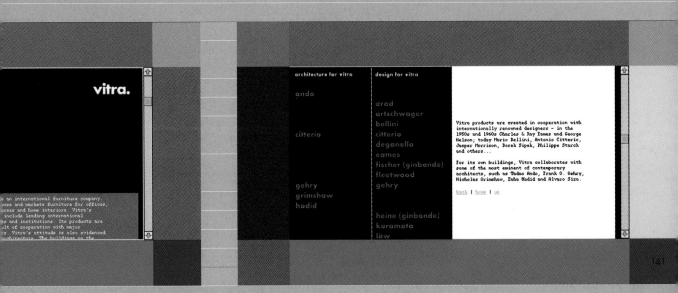

architecture for vitra | design for vitra

ando

    arad
    artschwager
    bellini
citterio   citterio
    deganello
    eames
    fischer (ginbande)
    fleetwood
gehry   gehry
grimshaw
hadid

    heine (ginbande)
    kuramata
    löw

Vitra products are created in cooperation with internationally renowned designers – in the 1950s and 1960s Charles & Ray Eames and George Nelson; today Mario Bellini, Antonio Citterio, Jasper Morrison, Borek Sipek, Philippe Starck and others...

For its own buildings, Vitra collaborates with some of the most eminent of contemporary architects, such as Tadao Ando, Frank O. Gehry, Nicholas Grimshaw, Zaha Hadid and Alvaro Siza.

back | home | up

141

DESIGN VIRTUAL IDENTITY

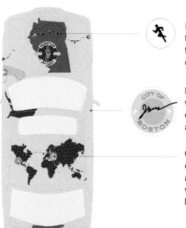

Icons show how the Torch bearers traveled to each city.

Host cities are honored with signatures of distinct politicians and public figures.

Olympic Games originating in Athens and arrives in LA, where the Torch Relay began.

States are mapped across the surface structure of the vehicle.

142

website design
project no: 035824
HcVN Website prototype v3.2

The World's Healthcare Village Network is a community of Medical and Healthcare professionals and organizations, creating global unity in its industry through technology. Initiating this idea is creating the corporate identity for HcVN. In its footsteps is the HcVN website. Through navigational and information design, Spire brings to life a directory of resources for the Telemedical field.

2

surface design
project no: 035857
BMW Olympic Signature Car

The BMW Olympic Signature Car utilitizes the ideas of a "Word Map" in documenting the 1996 Olympic Torch Relay. The Relay began in Los Angeles and traveled through over 200 host cities and ended in Atlanta. The Signature Car traveled with it. Each city is "mapped" across the surface structure of the vehicle. Currently the Signature Car is on display at the BMW Art Car Museum (Centrium) in Spartanburg, SC.

143

 back   next ▶

project
spire bmw
type
Helvetica Black, 12pt, 14pt, 21pt, 16opt

comment
This example has the appropriate column width, large type, and sufficient line spacing. The tracking could have been more generous. Normally, the secondary color magenta is not suitable for use on the screen because of its color intensity. But, as a single line against an achromatic background, it is perfectly suitable for use as an eye-catcher.

surface design

BMW Signature Car

Lichtfabrik

project
erco
type
Rotis/titel, Geneva or Arial 10pt.

DESIGN WEKEMANN & SCHÖLZ

144

topical

Projects
Airport

Sta
Arch
Light
Wash

Rare
desig
at St
ceilin
Uplig
of th
ceilin
below
comp
apar
arch
manu

Work in progress

The following pages provide information
on our current designs and projects. There
will be constant up-dates on developments
in these areas.
August 97

more

Projects

in Menu
utsche Version

We make light work

In the following pages we have selected
several projects to show exceptional
examples of effective correctly designed
lighting. Although we have drawn
projects from very different areas, we can
only give an indication of the variety of
lighting effects here. If you are interested
in more specific information, please write
to us.

comment

About 40 characters per line and clearly - structured paragraphs make these
pages very easy to read. White and different shades of gray create a
pleasant contrast which is not too strong. This example shows that a gray
background – broken up on some pages by screen color areas – is not
necessarily boring. Here, in the presentation of a lighting company, its
neutrality is particularly suitable. Even the yellow key words are effective in
this context.

145

t, London
and Partners, London
ude and Danielle Engle,

s have the opportunity to
rom scratch, as occurred
ncept of the "illuminating
ped for the airport.
lled in the cross-joints
llars illuminating the
ected light, the floor
ormly. This highly
pillars are 36 metres
se co-operation between
designer and luminaire

nsted Airport

Links

comment

The headlines attract a great deal of attention because of the drastic blooming of the white, bold type. Blooming can be used like this for short headlines. The black body texts are set effectively on an orange background to avoid blooming; the blue on the following page appears less interesting than the orange, and it weakens the effect of the photographs.

DESIGN MME CC CORPORATE COMMUNICATIONS

project
VH 1
type
Arial,
News Gothic Bd BT

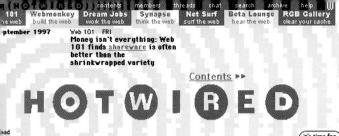

[(HOTWIRED)] contents members threads chat search archive help

101 | Webmonkey | Dream Jobs | Synapse | Net Surf | Beta Lounge | RGB Gallery
e web | build the web | work the web | think the web | surf the web | hear the web | clear your cache

September 1997   Web 101   FRI
Money isn't everything: Web 101 finds shareware is often better than the shrinkwrapped variety

Contents ►►

HOTWIRED

Net Surf   FRI
Joey Anuff on CNET's swerve from techheads to newbies: Mass speaks louder than niche

it's time for the meeting!

Synapse
Tune in Monday to hear VR guru Jaron Lanier's lecture from the New Media Minds conference

Synapse   FRI
Libertarianism aims to stay the hand of "nanny government" – is that so immature?

Webmonkey   THU
If you want to say e, francais or inlé! on the

Webmonkey   TUE
Emily Hobson loves XSSI

DESIGN ANNA M^cMILLAN, SABINE MESSNER

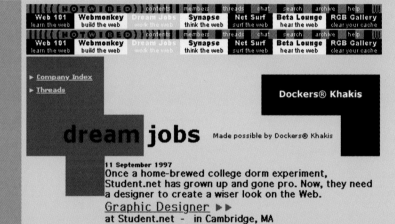

[(HOTWIRED)] contents members threads chat search archive help

Web 101 | Webmonkey | Dream Jobs | Synapse | Net Surf | Beta Lounge | RGB Gallery
learn the web | build the web | work the web | think the web | surf the web | hear the web | clear your cache

[(HOTWIRED)] contents members threads chat search archive help

Web 101 | Webmonkey | Dream Jobs | Synapse | Net Surf | Beta Lounge | RGB Gallery
learn the web | build the web | work the web | think the web | surf the web | hear the web | clear your cache

► **Company Index**
► **Threads**

Dockers® Khakis

dream jobs   Made possible by Dockers® Khakis

11 September 1997
Once a home-brewed college dorm experiment, Student.net has grown up and gone pro. Now, they need a designer to create a wiser look on the Web.
Graphic Designer ►►
at Student.net - in Cambridge, MA

9 September 1997
Prospecting for content
Organizer / Researcher ►
at American Civil
Liberties Union

project
hotwired
type
Verdana, 36pt and 7pt

comment
As a result of the fresh turquoise shade of the background, this
page looks very attractive (especially appropriate as it deals with
"dream jobs"). The body text in black is in a larger
type size so that the type is not overwhelmed by the background.
The comparison of black type on a light yellow background with
light yellow type of the same size on a turquoise background
shows that colors with a similar brightness, in this case turquoise
and light yellow, are difficult to read in combination, especially in
smaller type sizes. Whereas the small yellow type almost
disappears, the small black type can still be read. If turquoise is
used as the type color on a magenta background, it will create
a strong flickering effect – but in this case it is justified because it
is meant to stand out.

comment
The wide text line is acceptable here because it runs over only three lines.

project
fsb
type
Trade Gothic Light, 12pt

 FSB

Franz Schneider
Brakel GmbH+Co
Nieheimer Straße 38
33034 Brakel
Germany
Phone : (++49) 52 72 - 60 80
Fax : (++49) 52 72 - 60 83 00
e-mail : info@fsb.de

Welcome to the world of FSB. The door handle with which you have just accessed this page is based on a model designed by the Austrian philosopher Ludwig Wittgenstein in mid-20s' Vienna. It was the prototype for the many similar models that followed.

 FSB publications

 Environmental
Measures at FSB

 e-mail to FSB

 Ordering the FSB Manual

 Handles

 The Hand Game

 Fraunhofer Institute

 Design Friends

Clear, smooth surfaces and an aerodynamically optimized form: the design of the Audi AI2 is oriented to the future. Its taut surfaces and eye-catching edges point to the influence of airship engineering. The result: a unique, confident appearance. The concept: the maximum use of space combined with minimum space requirements. Aerodynamic lines and a discreet rear spoiler produce a sensationally low cd rating of 0.25. And cleverly designed details improve the car's ergonomic qualities and comfort.

We are not just concerned about quantitative values but emotional ones as well: having fun driving and experiencing both function and beauty. That's why the AI2 doesn't look like other cars. Just like the Audi of tomorrow's world.

Visions

Visions are born of passion

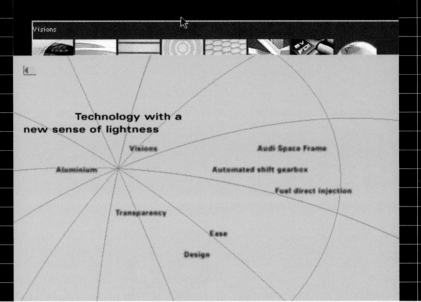

Technology with a new sense of lightness

Visions

Aluminium

Audi Space Frame

Automated shift gearbox

Fuel direct injection

Transparency

Ease

Design

DESIGN METADESIGN PLUS

visions   models   service   facts   news

models

Audi A8
Audi A6
Audi A4
Audi Cabriolet   Audi A3
Audi S4   Audi S8
Environment   Design   Safety

map | help | locator

Models

Design

Accessories
must be practical

The concept behind the A12 has been implemented even in
the tiniest details of its construction with lightness and
high-quality design reflected in its exclusive accessories.
For example the picnic basket with a built-in folding table
where a glass top matches the roof construction in its
transparency and colours. Or the somewhat different
buggy: its ultra-light, fold-away titanium frame can be
fastened to the rear seat and a child seat mounted on the
frame - in no time at all.

The interior of the A12 offers plenty of space for four
people. The vehicle concept makes it possible. Passengers
sit around 10 cm higher than in a normal compact car.
That gives the driver a better view and backseat
passengers more head- and legroom. The result is a much
more comfortable ride and an impressive experience of
roominess - despite considerably reduced exterior
dimensions.

But that's not all: we even tailor-made a set of cases to
fit the false bottom of the luggage compartment. Here,
too, the design language of the A12 is expressed in the
shape of the case handles - matching that of the door

Do you believe
is what you see?

What is the limit?

How does the journey
become the destination?

Visions begin
with questions

What engages you?

What way are
you going?

Where do you
drive tomorrow?

visions   models   service   facts   news

The Audi S8:
Feel the difference
without showing it

Dynamic, but controlled. Responsive, but
not aggressive. The Audi S8 is the superior
alternative to the sports car. You can
expect more from such an extraordinary
automobile: more performance, more
safety, more luxury.

The Audi S8 not only fascinates with the spectacular
unleashing of power from its V8 engine, but also with
its supreme handling, permanent 4-wheel-drive, and
its luxurious equipment and trim. Most of all, it
convinces with its charisma and conscious
understatement: the Audi S8 is a saloon that is built to
impress - yourself most of all.

map | help | locator   Audi A8

project
audi
type
Univers Bold Extended 12pt, 14pt
Geneva 9pt (mac), Arial 9pt (dos)
comment
Black type on a white background works
in this case because there is just one eye-
catcher and the viewer therefore stays on
this web page for only a short time. It is
noticeable that blurred type is used
deliberatly to create a three-dimensional
appearance.

White type on a black background is an
advantage for reading a longer text block
on the screen, and this text block is
clearly structured into paragraphs.
The gray sub-heading fits harmoniously
into the overall design of this page and
does not conflict with other elements, for
example, the photographs.

INDEX

153

LITERATURE

Code x
Micha Schaub
DuMont Buchverlag
Cologne, 1992

Die Macht der Farben
Harald Braem
Wirtschaftsverlag Langen-Müller/Herbig
Munich, 1985

Digitale Schriften
Darstellungen und Formate
Peter Karow
Springer Verlag
Berlin, 1992

Farben in Religion, Gesellschaft,
Kunst und Psychotherapie
Ingrid Riedel
Kreuz Verlag
Stuttgart, 1983

formdiskurs
Verlag form
Frankfurt, 3,II, 1997

Mensch und Farbe
Heinrich Frieling
Wilhelm Heine Verlag
Munich, 1988

The art of human computer interface design
Brenda Laurel
Addison Wisley Publication Company Inc.
1990

Typographie
Otl Aicher
Ernst & Sohn Verlag
Berlin, 1988

Typo und Layout
Vom Zeichenfall zum Screendesign
Cyrus Dominik Khazaeli
Rowolth Taschenbuch Verlag
Reinbek/Hamburg, 1995

Typographie Schrift Lesbarkeit
Hans Rudolf Bosshard
Verlag Niggli
Switzerland/Lihtenstein, 1996

DESIGNER   155

Examples

Body type, Sub-headings, Headlines **The Sans 3-Light**
Body type on pages 54–67 **Joanna MT**
highlighting typeface **The Sans 7-Bold**

TYPEFACES